JESUS:
The Death and Resurrection of God

Donald G. Dawe

John Knox Press
ATLANTA

Library of Congress Cataloging in Publication Data

Dawe, Donald G.
  Jesus : the death and resurrection of God.

  Bibliography; p.
  Includes index.
  1. Jesus Christ—Person and offices.
2. Christianity and other religions. I. Title.
BT202.D36   1985   232   85-5192
ISBN 0-8042-0527-2

© copyright John Knox Press 1985
10 9 8 7 6 5 4 3 2 1
Printed in the United States of America
John Knox Press
Atlanta, Georgia 30365

Preface

Despite pious intimations to the contrary, theology books do not drop from heaven. Instead they often have a long history of their own before they come into print. Such is the case with this book. Its origins lie in the past, when as a young faculty member I found myself teaching in a liberal arts college. I came to this post after some years in the pastorate and from graduate study at Union Theological Seminary in New York. With my new-found colleagues at Macalester College, I felt at times strangely unprepared to deal with their most persistent questions and keenly felt interests. My theological education had been at a school renowned for its commitment to interpreting the Christian faith to the modern world. Yet in the midst of a modern liberal arts college, I found myself presented with questions for which I had little comprehension and few answers. No longer was the field of discourse set by fellow scholars in biblical studies, theology, and church history. Now my colleagues were chemists, biologists, psychologists, philosophers, linguists, and historians. True, many of my students were struggling with the transition from the piety received at home to a faith viable in their new intellectual world. In dealing with this I was on familiar ground. But this was not the only problem with which I had to deal. Students and fellow teachers were concerned not just with Christianity but with a host of other religious options or no religion at all. Two things became clear to me. My theology had to deal with the revolution in scientific thought amid which we lived, and it also had to deal with the religious pluralism of our world. I knew that I had intended for some time to do a book on the person and work of Christ. My stay at Macalester College taught me that the confession of Jesus Christ as Lord had to be made in a new and far wider context than that of which I had ever dreamt.

Constructively, this book has grown while I have been on the faculty of Union Theological Seminary in Virginia. My colleagues and students have pressed upon me the high claims of Christian faithfulness and of the Reformed tradition. Theology must have a focus. Theology must wrestle with the questions raised by the world about it, yet it must wrestle with them from the perspective of a faith brought to expression in a theological tradition. The commitment of this community to biblical interpretation and the history of theology has given focus to my attempt to witness to what God is doing in the world today. Years of teaching and living, working and praying in this community have shaped this book around the reality of Jesus Christ.

There is always a tension when we seek to relate the unfolding story of humankind and its religious quest to the confession of faith in God as Father, Son, and Holy Spirit. This book is not an attempt to abolish that tension. It is written in the attempt to look more deeply into the mystery of how God deals with us. The book is written out of the conviction that Christian faith is a mystery but not an absurdity.

The scope of this book has broadened through my teaching at the Punjabi University, Patiala, India, and at the University of Jos, Nigeria. Here amid students and colleagues the traditions of Hinduism, Sikhism, Buddhism, Islam, and African traditional religion came to life. They were no longer distant voices attracting my attention but insistent realities with which each day I was called to deal. My gracious reception by His Holiness, the Dalai Lama and his staff at Dharamsala, India, and by Harbans Singh at the Guru Gobind Singh Bhavan, Patiala, India, gave insights to which I trust I have been faithful.

It is always difficult to name all of those who have had a share in any work. A long succession of teachers, students, friends, and family, especially Joanna Dawe, have shared in this work, but thanks must be given now to those close at hand. Particular thanks are due to Ross Mackenzie, a colleague and friend whose help with technical questions and as a sounding board for my opinions has been of the greatest importance. Thanks are also due to Union Theological Seminary in Virginia, through whose generous leave policy and support for faculty publications this book has been made possible. Martha Aycock, John Trotti, and the staff of our library have been tireless in making its resources available for my work. Sally Hicks, through her patient and painstaking work, has made the manuscript intelligible and accurate—no small blessing since it came from an author so uncertain on a typewriter. The skill of Nancy Hardesty as an editor and her knowledge as a historian have clarified insights and refined documentation.

Donald G. Dawe
Union Theological Seminary in Virginia

Contents

This book is for
Joanna and Phil, Stephen and Donna
that they and their generation may
catch the vision of Jesus
whose way is life.

PART I

Reasons for Hope

Where Is the Messianic Age?

"If Jesus was the Messiah, where is the messianic age?" This was the question addressed to me by Rabbi Joshua Sperka as we sat in his study. We were surrounded by learned commentaries and had the Hebrew text of the book of Isaiah open before us. I was a seminary student at that time, and had come fresh from a course on the book of Isaiah. We had studied with great care the Servant songs of Second Isaiah, especially the fourth song, Isaiah 52:13– 53:12. In this song the author of Second Isaiah had written with words of fire of the Servant of Yahweh whose suffering and death "make many to be accounted righteous." The song is one of suffering and death but also of triumph. The Servant will receive from the Lord "a portion with the great." The suffering of the Servant, which by the standards of the world was irrevocable loss, had become through the power of God a means of salvation for the world. "By his knowledge shall the righteous one, my servant, make many to be accounted righteous." The way of suffering love is triumphant. But who is this Servant? Can we know the one through whom suffering love is to triumph?

My fundamentalist upbringing had long before acquainted me with the Christian interpretation of the fourth Servant song as a prophecy of Jesus, his death and resurrection. It had once seemed all so clear and evident. Was this not another proof, perhaps the supreme proof, of how prophecy had been fulfilled in Jesus the Messiah? My introduction to the historical-critical study of the Bible had unsettled the certainty the argument from fulfilled prophecy had once given me. In our seminary class we had wrestled long and hard with the question of the identity of the Servant. Was the Servant the people of Israel, the prophet himself, some unknown sufferer of the exile, or someone yet to come? I knew the many answers to this question given by biblical scholars. But my quest was unfulfilled. So one afternoon I went for a conversation with a neighbor and long-time friend, Rabbi Joshua Sperka. I went to the Rabbi for help in resolving a problem of learned exegesis. I came away from our conversation with a question that has haunted me ever since: "If Jesus was the Messiah, where is the messianic age?"

Rabbi Joshua Sperka and his wife had fled ghetto life in Poland as the specter of Nazism was rising in Europe. They had settled in a lower-middle-class neighborhood on the west side of Detroit, where Rabbi Sperka was the spiritual leader of Beth David Synagogue. The Sperkas were our neighbors in what today we would call an "ecu-menical" neighborhood although that word was unknown to us at the time. Our house was equidistant between Beth David Synagogue and the Roman Catholic Church of the Visitation. My family's church, Dexter Boulevard Baptist Church, was a few miles away. One of the affinities between the Sperkas and my family was our common devotion to a legalistic piety and our deep reverence for the Scriptures. Granted that we followed different canons of Scriptures and observed Sabbath on different days of the week, we found a closeness to the Sperkas that we did not have with our Roman Cath-olic neighbors. Although they were regular in going to mass, our Roman Catholic neighbors seemed never to grasp the importance of the Bible nor the desire of God to set aside one of the days of the week as holy. They returned from mass to wash their cars or cut their lawns, which we were certain was displeasing to God.

We also knew that the Sperkas were looking for the coming of the Messiah. While we believed that Jesus is already Messiah, we knew full well that God had not turned from the covenant people of old. The promised salvation would yet come to Israel. The details of how this would happen remained unclear although we thought we found some clues in reading Daniel, Ezekiel, and Revelation. In retrospect the dispensationalist theology that supported this convic-tion seems riddled with contradiction. But it did have one positive effect. We knew that we were partners in waiting. The Sperkas were waiting for the coming of the Promised One who would usher in the messianic age of peace. We were waiting for a coming also. It was to be the coming again of Jesus to establish the kingdom of God. So it was very natural for me to seek out Rabbi Sperka during a vacation after my second year in seminary. In this time of waiting we pondered together on the Suffering Servant of the Lord.

The Rabbi brought down from his bookshelves great tomes of learned interpretation and pondered them with me. I listened to the faith of Israel and then raised the question of my own faith. "What sense," I asked the Rabbi, "can you make out of the Christian claim that the Suffering Servant of the Lord is Jesus whom we confess to be the Messiah?" He paused for a moment that seemed freighted with the weight of eternity. Then he said, "I can see how you Christians can believe that Jesus was the Suffering Servant of the Lord. But if he was the Messiah, where is the messianic age?" Rabbi Sperka could well ask the question because his family and that of his wife had perished in the Holocaust. Where is the messianic age? If the Messiah is to bring life and peace and joy, how could the tragedy of the present exist in the time after the Messiah has come?

The Rabbi's question launched me on a quest, the full dimensions of which I only dimly perceived at the time. I knew the answers that Christians make to such questions. The Christ who came once in humility, we say, will come again in glory to establish the kingdom of God. Then there will be full justice and perfect peace. This is how Christians have sought to answer the Rabbi's question. But put in just that way, it is not a satisfactory answer. How can we make such extravagant claims for Messiah Jesus when the traces of his presence are so thin, and the power of his love so fleeting? A religious vision that thrusts salvation into an unspecified future inevitably collapses because we human beings live in the present. We may have future hopes and memories of the past, but if the present is drained of meaning we are bereft and lost.

Elie Wiesel (b. 1928) spoke of the dilemma of unfulfilled hopes in his report of a conversation he had with an aged Hasidic Jew who lived in a town in Hungary whose Jewish population had been killed in the Holocaust. The aged Hasid had escaped and was living out his remaining days in an empty synagogue. When asked what hopes and what faith sustained him, he replied that he no longer had any. He said to Wiesel, "Even if Messiah came today, it would already be too late." The price in suffering and death was already so great that no future act of deliverance, no balancing of the scales of justice, no renewal of the wellsprings of hope could make faith in God the Lord possible.

In contrast, Christians claim a finality and completeness for the salvation given in Jesus Christ. Yet the world, or even the church, knows nothing of this completeness. We live amid the powers of sin and death. We see the threat of the power of sin and death writ large for us in the crises of ecology, overpopulation, and nuclear war. And we see this power in the personal tragedy that breaks into human life. A DNA molecule fails to connect properly, a bit of genetic material is missing, a treatment-resistant virus invades the system, and where there had been health and strength and hope, there is tragic disability, suffering, and death. In this kind of a world, how do we relate the finality of salvation in Jesus Christ to the fragmentary and elusive presence of that salvation that we see around us? Unless we can find some new vision by which to form our faith, we shall find ourselves slowly but inexorably withdrawing our faith in Jesus Christ as Lord of all. As Christians, we claim we live by hope, hope in the coming completion of the work that Jesus began almost two thousand years ago. But if that hope is not to wither, we must be able "to account for the hope" that is within us (1 Peter 3:15).

Looking at the Foundations

My conversation with Rabbi Sperka, although unknown to me at the time, was the fulfillment of words spoken by Franz Rosenzweig (1886–1929), one of the great interpreters of the importance of Judaism for Christianity. In dialogue with his Christian friend Eugen Rosenstock-Huessy, Rosenzweig said, "You who live in an *ecclesia triumphans* have need of a servant . . . , which when you think you already enjoy God in bread and wine, cries out to you: 'Master, be mindful of the last things.' "[1] Israel, in the person of Rabbi Sperka, had been a servant of God to me to call me to face again "the last things"—those aspects of my faith that touched on the final victory of God over evil. In systematic theology it is called eschatology. Yet the concern here is with more than a particular "head of doctrine." It is the need to look at the heart of Christian faith, faith in Jesus Christ, and ask what we confess when we call him Lord of all. Too often we Christians have settled for limited definitions of the all of which Jesus is Lord. We have settled for defining salvation as relief from psychic tensions, the resolution of social problems, strengthening national interests, or enlarging ecclesiastical power. To look to "the last things" means to look to the whole human story and confess a faith that embraces all space and time.

Christians confess that illumination of the meaning of life and victory over its distortion are given by faith in Jesus. To know him in faith is not simply to have information about him, no matter how good and true that information may be. To have faith in Jesus Christ is to "have life, and have it abundantly." But for increasing numbers this faith is not so much a reality as a wistful hope. The question asked by Rabbi Sperka is not just a Jewish question; it is a basic human question. Not everyone would put it in the distinctively Jewish way that the Rabbi did. "If Jesus was the Messiah, where is the messianic age?" Instead some might say, "What does faith in Christ mean amid not only the tragedy and contingency of human life but also amid its boredom and blank confusion?" It does little good to tell people to look at the church. There is good in the church. Yet there is also a terrible gap between the good we claim for ourselves and the good that is actually lived. We church people tend to make such extraordinary claims about such ordinary people. If we are the messianic people, where is the new age? While we are always ready to accept facile explanations of our failures and follies, it should not surprise us that those outside the church do not find our explanations convincing.

Our witness to Jesus Christ is stymied because our proclamation of him is riddled by contradictions. There is a glaring disproportion between what we claim for salvation in Christ and how we now experience that salvation. There is a disproportion between the universality of our claims for Jesus Christ and the limited place of Christianity in a religiously plural world. The church suffers from a crisis of hope because for too long we have been unable to deal with the tragic. It is as if we believe that we can be raised with Christ without having been crucified with Christ. We act as if Christianity were already the religion of all humankind, while it is a particular religion that can claim only a minority of the world's population. Strident reaffirmations of the finality and universality of Jesus Christ are of no effect. No amount of the emotionally charged dogmatism of a renewed fundamentalism can bring authenticity to our witness. We cannot wall off the world in its tragedy and complexity to preserve our witness to Jesus. The good news is that we do not have to. Christ is already Lord of all. Our institutions, our power, our influence, not even our faith can make him Lord. Our task is to trace Christ's presence and respond to his love. But to be faithful in this task we dare not exclude the human tragedies and religious complexities all around us. What we need is a new vision of Jesus Christ as Lord. The question is how we go about finding that vision.

The church has formed its vision of Jesus and the salvation given in him by relating three elements: (1) the witness of Scripture, both Old and New Testaments, to Jesus Christ; (2) the traditions of those who have responded to Jesus Christ and have reflected on his meaning, particularly as found in the great creeds and confessions, such as Nicaea and Chalcedon; and (3) the ways in which people understand themselves and the world of which they are a part.

The vision of Jesus as Lord and Christ occurs when these three elements come together to bring power and illumination to people of faith. The relationship of Scripture, tradition, and world that discloses Jesus Christ is not arrived at mechanically; nor is it determined by church authorities or academics. It is a gift of grace bestowed by the Holy Spirit. When, in the power of the Spirit, the witness of Scripture, tradition, and our modes of self-understanding come into correlation with one another, revelation occurs. They form a configuration of revelation that allows people to see through them to the reality of God in Christ. When these elements are in contradiction, they give no transparency into the divine. We perceive them only as opaque and dissonant.

At certain times in the history of the church the relationship of

Scripture, tradition, and world has provided visions of Jesus Christ. The Fathers of the early church wrestled to make a faithful witness to Christ in the cultural and religious world of Greco-Roman antiquity. In the High Middle Ages, Aquinas and the Schoolmen defended and reformulated the faith in theology and piety. In the Reformation of the sixteenth century, Luther, Calvin, and their contemporaries brought Scripture back into relation to tradition to find a vision of salvation in Christ.

By the early nineteenth century, piety and theology were brought into a new pattern of revelation in the theology of Schleiermacher and the great teachers of Protestant liberalism. In this century Barth and the neo-orthodox theologians, with prophetic zeal, brought together Scripture, tradition, and contemporary life into a startling new configuration that revitalized faith. But for many people today there is no revelatory configuration. Rather they experience dissonance between the witness of Scripture, traditional piety, and churchly teaching and their understanding of themselves and the ways of the world of which they are a part. They no longer see Scripture and church as providing a window through which the light of revelation can shine to give meaning and hope. For some this opaqueness has been so persistent that the question of faith in Jesus Christ has passed into oblivion.

It is not possible to slip back behind the complexities of history to some pre-Christian Jesus. As modern biblical scholarship has made so clear, we have no access to a simple, uninterpreted Jesus because such a person never existed. Nor is it possible to ignore the vast literature of Christology, ancient and modern. We are already surrounded "by so great a cloud of witnesses" that to ignore them is to condemn ourselves to repeat their errors without benefit of their truth. But an encyclopedic history of doctrine is not what we need. Rather what we need is to look afresh at Jesus and the struggle to know and confess him through this faith. What we need is analysis of how Jesus is known and of what facilitates or blocks the confession of him as Lord and Christ.

The search is an intellectual one carried on by the techniques of historical, philosophical, and theological analysis. Yet such a search is done in the power of the Spirit. If it is possible to reach a new revelatory configuration for this time, it will be a gift of the Spirit. Coming to know Jesus Christ is not the result of human wisdom or power or goodness. It is not "of the flesh." It is "of the Spirit." Our intellectual analysis is a gift, offered up in the hope that it will be empowered by the Spirit.

1

Faith and Thought

Clarity and Uncertainty

Viewing the early growth of Christology, the historian Edward Rochie Hardy (b. 1908) characterized the situation at the end of the third century with an optimistic phrase. The church, he said, had reached "clarity in general principles but uncertainty in details."[1] The intellectual situation today can best be characterized by reversing the phrase. Now we face uncertainty in general principles but have some clarity in details. The Christological titles of the New Testament have been analyzed against their background in the history of religions. The unfolding Christologies of the New Testament and the early Church Fathers have been given minute study. The theologians and Council Fathers of Nicaea and Chalcedon are known to us as their positions unfolded in the complex interplay of piety and politics. The Christologies of the Reformers, their scholastic interpreters, and their left-wing critics are explicated in scholarly monographs. Even the tumultuous Christologies of the nineteenth century are being rendered compassable, despite their multivolume German splendor, by a growing literature of interpretation. Clarity in details grows apace. This growth has been not only the work of historians and biblicists. Theologians in modern times cannot be thought remiss in proliferating insights into the person and work of Christ.

From the beginnings of modern theology, the Christological doctrines have been recast under the impact of many philosophical schools. In the nineteenth and early twentieth centuries, neo-Kantians created the liberal Christologies based on "the historical Jesus," while Hegelian speculation created the Christ of modernism.

Personalism became the basic motif in the Christologies of the mediating theologians of that period as they tried to knit together confessional theologies and modern thought.[2] Contemporary Christologies
have been developed on the basis of existentialism, process philosophy, linguistic analysis, liberation theology, and phenomenology.[3]
Since the advent of the radical theologies of "the death of God,"
interpretations of Jesus have been made from the perspectives of
humanistic Marxism and depth psychology.[4] Passionate thinkers,
speaking from within the movements for the liberation of Blacks,
women, and the nations of the Third World, have provided fresh
formulations of Jesus and his meaning. A recension of Christology
to rid it of its anti-Semitic implications has been made necessary by
the Holocaust.[5] The universality of Christ has been undergoing analysis in light of the non-Christian religious traditions.[6] However,
amid this proliferation of thought, no single interpretive scheme has
emerged to bring order among them. Lacking order, the multitude
of details has brought not clearer perception but deepening
uncertainty.

A Method in Disarray

Modern theological scholarship has oriented its constructive work by means of the historical method, as perfected in the
German universities of the nineteenth century.[7] When historical
method is used properly, the growth of historical details is supposed
to bring not confusion but ever greater clarity. In the historical
method a new theological position is to sum up all past developments and move the formulation of a doctrine to ever greater clarity.
The method is, according to Ernst Troeltsch (1865–1923), "to overcome history by history."[8] The confusions, misunderstandings, and
limitations of our particular time and place are to be overcome by
understanding how they relate to the past from which they have
emerged.

The results of scholarly research find their place in a scheme of
historical understanding that provides, in Troeltsch's wonderful
phrase, "a platform for new productive action." The preacher, the
teacher, as well as intelligent, serious-minded church members, are

supposedly dependent upon the historical theologian for guidance in matters of faith. By knowing the pattern of history, historicists claimed, the contemporary Christian will be able to give creative new direction to the preaching, liturgy, educational programs, and social actions of the church. Thus historical understanding will provide "a platform for new productive action." The promise of the historical method in theology was great. Its irony is in the disarray it has created. By the end of the twentieth century, many are ready to forsake historical method for new ideologies that combine theological conservatism and political nostalgia as the supposed "platform for new productive action" in the church. Where did things go astray?

For the historical method in theology to work, there has to be an agreed-upon context for reflection. Historical reflection functions as a basis for theology as long as there is wide agreement about what history is relevant and what historical evidence counts for or against theological positions. If there is a clearly defined and widely accepted context for historical reflection, then such reflection will provide the adjustments and refinements of doctrinal positions. If there is a clear spectrum of theological opinions, then there is hope for a progressive blending of colors into new theologies. Today, we are experiencing what Lonnie Kliever (b. 1931) has rightly called "the shattered spectrum" of Protestant theology.

The most evident symptom of the breakdown of the historical method is the persistent reduction it has produced in what can be said or believed about Jesus. When compared with the classical Christologies of Catholicism and scholastic Protestantism, or even those of nineteenth-century modernism, contemporary Christology is sharply limited in its affirmations. Despite the efforts to escape this reductionism, the Christological affirmations have been progressively eroded. The doctrine of the human and divine natures has been declared untenable for philosophical, ethical, and biblical reasons. The nicely tuned arguments about the hypostatic union of the human and divine natures of Christ were not so much resolved as abandoned. The question of Jesus' God-consciousness or the extent of the divine self-emptying in the Incarnation has slipped out of the awareness of contemporary theology. Such puzzles, it is argued, arise from philosophical misunderstandings or historical misperceptions. People who live in the clean, cool world of hard-edged scientific technology, we are assured, have no interest in such conundrums. So, paradoxically, the passion to make Jesus relevant to more and more of life is contradicted by our shrinking ability to know him or interpret his importance. Austin Farrer (1904–68) once asked whether we were not in danger of "freeing the Gospel from its fetters by amputating its limbs."[9] An underlying pattern of thought is at work here, like a Procrustean bed, shortening all thought to its own dimensions. Michel Foucault (1926–1984), the French structuralist, puts the case in its most extreme form:

> What counts in the things said by men is not so much what they may have thought or the extent to which these things represent their thoughts, as that which systematizes them from the outset, thus making them thereafter endlessly accessible to new discourses and open to the task of transforming them.[10]

Is it possible to identify this pattern and move beyond its limitations?

The Exchanging of Metaphors

The context of theological reflection is derived from root metaphors by which thought is organized. These root metaphors are basic models or pictures of reality by which people sort out experience and organize their reflections on Scripture and tradition to create a specific theology. Various metaphors have dominated Christological thought in its development. These metaphors are not the sole sources of a Christology. Rather they function to organize data from Scripture, tradition, and common human experience. These metaphors are not abstract a priori principles that can be stated with logical precision. Rather root metaphors are locked up in pictures or stories through which reflection is organized. They are fundamental ways of encompassing in finite, human words a vision that transcends and shapes all else. Such root metaphors establish the logic and determine the limitations within which a particular Christology functions. Getting at these root metaphors is difficult and admittedly abstract.

In the course of history, Christian faith has been faced by two definitive changes in its articulation of the person and work of Jesus. The first of these changes came at the very origins of Christianity when the church found itself propelled by its missionary impulse from the world of Palestinian Judaism, within which it was born, into the world of Greco-Roman antiquity. The second change came as Christianity, now the religion of the Western world, faced the challenge of modernity with its scientific worldview and the immense empowering of humankind by its technology. Today through historical scholarship, we can look back at the first great adaptation of Christian faith to a new context in great detail. The movement of Christianity from being a religion shaped by the Jewish-apocalyptic vision to that of hellenistic-Gnostic sources gave rise, through the formulations of the Councils of Nicaea and Chalcedon, to the classical tradition in Christology.

The council decisions of the early church on the divinity and humanity of Christ created a context that dominated Christological reflection until the beginnings of modernity in the Renaissance and Enlightenment. No matter how wide their variations, the Christologies of this classical tradition had an underlying unity because they shared basic visions of Jesus' relation to God and to the whole of humankind. By contrast, the Christologies formulated in response to modernity are informed by a different logic. They too possess an underlying unity although their details assume a bewildering multiplicity. This unity is harder to perceive. Yet there is a clear and decisive modern pattern to what can be thought and believed about Jesus.

The differences between classical and modern Christologies are based on an exchange of root metaphors. The metaphors that have shaped reflection in the classical tradition of Christology have been replaced by different ones in the modern tradition. By identifying the dominant metaphor of each tradition, it will be possible not only to illumine the present stage of Christological reflection but to move to new possibilities.

In making the distinction between a "classical" and a "modern" tradition in Christology, it should be clear that no point in time completely divides the two. Modernity has its roots and early definitions in the sixteenth through the eighteenth centuries. However, this period does not mark the end of the classical tradition. Classical Christologies have been found subsequently among some of the theologians of the Roman Catholic, Anglican, Orthodox, Reformed, and Lutheran churches.[11] In fact, this book will argue that a fresh appropriation of the root metaphor of the classical tradition opens the way to a new Christology.

The Classical Tradition

The highest priority on the theological agenda of early Christianity was formulating its confession of Jesus as the Christ. Theology got its start as Christians became increasingly aware of the tensions between the Jewish-apocalyptic worldview, by which they first confessed their faith, and the hellenistic-Gnostic worldview of the gentiles to whom their mission had sent them. Two problems quickly became evident: the problem of time and the problem of language. Already within the first century, the church had to deal with the problem of time. The earliest Christians believed that they were living in a brief interim between the resurrection of Jesus and his return in glory to establish the kingdom of God. Jesus was confessed as the Son of Man who had come once in humility but who would return with legions of angels to usher in the new age. Faith in Jesus and perseverance in his "Way" were the key to entry into the kingdom. Before the end of the first century, faith in the imminent coming of the kingdom of God was facing difficulty. The earliest traditions about Jesus had to be rethought and related to other visions of reality. Christians had to refocus their faith to face a long-range future.

The very success of the gentile mission brought to the church another crisis, the crisis of language. Having moved into the religious-cultural world of the Roman empire, Christians had to find new words to confess their faith. It was not simply that the time-frame of the Jewish-apocalyptic worldview was inadequate; its categories of thought were largely unintelligible in the gentile world. The problem was how to confess faith in Jesus without making him just another member of the pantheon of savior gods found in the mystery religions or in Gnosticism. This necessitated a massive reworking of terminology that often took the meaning of words through a virtual turnabout. This reconceptualization dominated the Christology of the patristic age. In all this, the church was caught between necessity and threat. The necessity was to make its witness to Jesus Christ clear and compelling in a religious-cultural context that was alien to its origins. The threat was that in this reinterpretation the saving power of the gospel would be lost.

Four councils marked the summation of the Christological doctrine developed by the church in its struggle to confess Christ in the ethos of Greco-Roman antiquity. The Council Fathers of Nicaea (325), Constantinople (381), Ephesus (431), and Chalcedon (451) gave classical form to the basic Christological affirmations. From these councils came two confessional statements that gave shape to the liturgical and theological life of the church. The first is the creed of Nicaea, as enlarged and reaffirmed at Constantinople, that defined the relationship of Jesus Christ, the Son of God, to God the Father. Jesus Christ is confessed as being "of one substance [essence] with the Father" (Gr., *homoousion tō patri*). The immediate problem before the Council of Nicaea was the repudiation of the heresy of the Arians who wanted to confess Jesus as being Godlike (*homoiousion tō patri*) but not really sharing in the divine being.

However, the Nicaean definition reached far beyond that particular problem because it sealed on the mind of the church its central affirmation and its abiding problem. What God had done in Jesus Christ by becoming human was not something accidental or alien to God. Rather the enfleshing of the Son was the disclosure of the highest truth about God. To confess Jesus as "of one substance with the Father" is to confess that God is free to become human and yet not to become unlike deity. The Christian affirmation of incarnation means that God is not dealing with humankind at second hand through a chain of semidivine mediators. It is *God* who was in Christ reconciling the world to God and not some other (2 Cor. 5:19). Jesus is not a uniquely inspired person who brings the will of God to humankind. In Jesus, God is personally present. Hence, all that can be said of the self-sufficiency of God, of the divine omnipotence, omnipresence, and omniscience, has to be said in light of the fact that, in Jesus, God has been incarnated and in so doing has not ceased being God.

The definition of the divinity of Christ given at Nicaea opened in a new and more acute way the question of how to conceive his relationship to the rest of humankind. Ever since the struggle against the Gnostics, the church had maintained belief in the full reality of Jesus' humanity. The Council of Nicaea rejected any attempt to preserve the reality of Jesus' human nature by "scaling down," as it were, his divinity so as to allow for his humanity. The definitions that the church had made of both the divinity and humanity of Jesus had now to be related to one another. If the affirmations of Jesus' divinity and humanity were not actively related to one another, then the vision of Jesus would be betrayed into an absurdity. The church would end up with faith in someone who existed in two aspects, totally devoid of personal unity. At the Council of Ephesus, the church rejected Nestorian Christology. Nestorians affirmed the integrity of the divine and human natures in Jesus while insisting that they were related by the unity of the divine and human wills. While in Jesus the will of God was given full acceptance, the church insisted on a deeper, fuller way of linking the human and divine natures. Yet the exact way to formulate this link remained elusive. Finally, at Chalcedon, a formula emerged that did not resolve the mystery of the incarnation but defined the context in which this mystery is found. It is a formulary that has shaped Christological reflection ever since.

The Council Fathers at Chalcedon looked back to Nicaea and reaffirmed their faith in Jesus Christ as "of the same reality as God" the Father (*homoousion tō patri*). But then they extended the use of the technical term *homoousion* to include his humanness. He is "of the same reality as we are ourselves [*homoousion hēmin*] as far as his human-ness is concerned." From this basis the Definition of Chalcedon focuses on the mystery of incarnation itself:

> [We also teach] that we apprehend [*gnōridzomenon*] this one and only Christ—Son, Lord, only-begotten—in two natures [*duo physesin*]; [and we do this] without confusing the two natures [*asunkutōs*], without transmuting one nature into the other [*atreptōs*], without dividing them into two separate categories [*adiairetōs*], without contrasting them according

to area or function [*achōristōs*]. The distinctiveness of each nature is not nullified by the union. Instead, the "properties" [*idiotētos*] of each nature are conserved and both natures concur [*suntrechousēs*] in one "person" [*prosōpon*] and in one *hypostasis*.[12]

The classical tradition in Christology was set by the Chalcedonian formula: "two natures . . . in one person." The Definition of Chalcedon did not explain how God and humanity could be united in one person. Rather it set boundaries that made this question inescapable. In doing this, it reflected what stands at the heart of Christian faith: in Jesus Christ, God and humankind have been brought into a new relationship. It is a redemptive relationship in which the alienating powers of sin and death have been overcome. Intimacy has replaced alienation. In Jesus Christ, God expresses the divine freedom in love by becoming human without becoming unlike the divine essence. Moreover, this Jesus, in whom God has come, is a centered, fully human person.

Mystery and Absurdity

The Chalcedonian formula of "two natures . . . in one person" points to a mystery but not an absurdity. An absurdity is impenetrable to thought because there is contradiction at the heart of it. An absurdity is like a muddy pond. It is impenetrable to vision because there is obscurity in its very substance. By contrast, a mystery is like a deep pond of clear water. Vision cannot reach the bottom because of its depth, yet the water in the pond is clarity itself. The person of Christ, in the classical tradition, is a mystery, not an absurdity. Vision may penetrate it but never exhaust it. So to work within the classical tradition of Christology set by Nicaea and Chalcedon is not the end of thought or a substitute for thought. It is the context of thought. What the Chalcedonian formula of "two natures . . . in one person" pointed to was an act of union that the Greek Fathers called the *perichoresis*, "coinherence," of the divine and human.

The very terms within which the Definition of Chalcedon had been made pointed to the metaphor of coinherence. The "two natures" (*duo physesin*), human and divine, are not static, alien "things" that have to be forced together. The image behind the

Greek word *physis*, translated through the Latin *natura* as "nature," is that of the process of something emerging from the hidden. *"Physis"* is the characterization of the realm of that which arises and grows. A "nature" is not a static something but a power of being. In this sense, the patristic writers could use the term *physis* as a way of speaking about Jesus in his being as God and in his being as human. What they were rejecting was the notion that Jesus was God and an already existing human being joined together or that Jesus was part human and part divine. Rather in Jesus each nature does what is proper to it in communion with the other. The two natures interpenetrate one another yet do not become unlike themselves. There is coinherence of God and humankind. They form a hypostatic union which the classical Christologies characterized as based upon a "sharing of attributes" (*communicatio idiomatum*). The being of Jesus is that of a single person because the two natures coinhere.

This framework of classical Christology is found in the patristic theologians, the medieval Schoolmen, the Reformers, and their scholastic interpreters. It structured the Christology of the German- and English-speaking mediating theologians of the nineteenth and early twentieth centuries and emerges in the mature Christology of Barth. Anglican, Orthodox, and Roman Catholic theologians have shared in it also. This tradition is not a particular Christology but a common framework for reflection. No matter how successful or unsuccessful a particular theologian may have been in interpreting the tradition, the context remained the same. The study of Scripture, the refutation of heresy, or the confirming of piety brought to theologians a mass of data. These data were arranged in a pattern set by the metaphor of coinherence and hence came to clear focus.

The church made its confession of Jesus in two natures and one person because they knew Jesus as Redeemer. The classical tradition is not only concerned with the being of Jesus, a man of the first century, but with his power as Savior and Lord. The classical tradition links the person and work of Christ. This link is in the fact that Jesus, the first-century Palestinian Jew, was the one who became "both Lord and Christ" through whom forgiveness of sins is given (Acts 2:36–38). The Christian faith is not lived out of information about Jesus but by sharing his unique power of being. We are new creatures, as Paul repeatedly said, "in Christ." In faith Jesus' power of being becomes our power of being. As Philip Melanchthon (1497–1550) put it, "to know Christ is to know his benefits." To know his person is to know the source of being from which the faithful receive new life.

The Myth of the Ditch

The shift to modern Christological reflection was made by an exchange of metaphors from one of coinherence to one of separation. The modern tradition in Christology does not grow out of the reality of revelation in Jesus Christ; rather, it seeks to determine if such a revelation can actually take place. The classical tradition proceeds from the coinherence of God and humankind in Jesus while the modern tradition starts from the chasm between the divine and human and explores the possibility that in Christ this separation was overcome. Modern Christology is not the exploration of the coinherence of God and humankind already given in Jesus. It is but the search for some point of contact between history, the realm of human activity, and the transcendent, the realm of God.

In his tract *On the Proof of the Spirit and of Power*, Gotthold Ephraim Lessing (1729–81) expressed the root metaphor of modern Christology. It is a metaphor of disjunction that has dominated thinking about the relationship of God and humankind. As Lessing gave it literary expression, the metaphor became extended into a myth. It is the myth of the ditch. Lessing wrote of "the ugly broad ditch which I cannot get across, however often and however earnestly I have tried to make the leap."[13] The ditch is the separation of what Lessing called the "accidental truths of history" from the "necessary truths of reason." The events of human history, according to Lessing, cannot give us access to the realm of ultimate reality. Human existence and God are separated from one another by an "ugly broad ditch." History, the realm of human life, is contingent, accidental, and is known with only approximate accuracy. The truth about God, which is one of the "necessary truths of reason," cannot be given by historical events. At best, historical events may illustrate eternal truths but never establish them.

The problem is how to deal with the central affirmations of

Christian faith in such an intellectual setting. If the decisive revelation of God is given in the historical existence of Jesus—his life, death, and resurrection—then, "the accidental truths of history" are the disclosure of God. For Lessing, this is an impossibility because God exists in the realm of logically necessary truth. God is known with the certainty that human experience never gives. God is separate from the imperfectly known facts of history. There is no point at which they coinhere. Instead, an "ugly broad ditch" leaves human existence locked up in the contingent world of everyday life. Human beings may know the transcendent by reason and find it in moral values and spiritual aspirations. But there can be no interpenetration of the human and divine. In this context, the Christological question becomes whether any disclosure of God in history is possible. The modern question is whether Jesus Christ could be a link across "the ugly broad ditch." Thought does not move from the reality of revelation in Jesus Christ but from the question of its possibility. Unfortunately, the myth of the ditch has excluded any but a negative answer.

The history of modern Christology can be written as the exploration of Lessing's "ugly broad ditch," to see if there is any way to cross it. Immanuel Kant (1724–1804) identified the ditch unerringly. He saw the separation between "the phenomenal realm"—the sphere of everyday experience—and "the noumenal realm"—the sphere of ultimate reality which lies outside the powers of human thought. The ditch could only be crossed, Kant concluded, in the experience of ethical obligation which gives a limited but valid insight into God and ultimate reality. But then Kant adds, as if to leave his original analysis unsullied, that ethical obligation gives no real knowledge of God or the soul.[14] God is but a corollary of the human experience of ethical obligation. The ditch remained intact. Liberal Christologies based on Kantian thought probed the ethical and religious experience of humanity to find just how God could be known. It is through Jesus, the ethical-religious teacher, liberal Protestants concluded, and his ability to reinforce and enlarge human moral and spiritual character. But Jesus, the religious genius, does not reveal a transcendent God but only confirms the ethic of bourgeois idealism. Jesus is on our side of the ditch with only the thinnest thread of intuition relating him to the transcendent.

Georg W. F. Hegel (1770–1831) made a complex dialectical analysis of the myth of the ditch. In dialectical fashion, Hegel both affirmed and denied that the ditch could be crossed. He believed that the ditch could be crossed in pure thought, yet it has not been crossed historically. The human mind can reach the idea of *Gottmenschlichkeit*, the affirmation of the ultimate unity of God and humankind. This is the highest realization of all human religious searching. It is an ideal realized philosophically by rational reflection. However, Jesus, as he actually lived historically, was only the practical embodiment, the *Vorstellung*, a pictorial representation of the ideal of the divine humanity.[15] For Hegel, the legends, myths, and stories that make up the history of Jesus are a kind of picture language that express for the religious mind the truth that is known in full rational clarity only to the philosophical mind. The reconciliation of God with humankind is not established by the life, death, and resurrection of Jesus. They are already reconciled in principle. The legends of historical reconciliation through Jesus are but half-real pictures needed for those who have not yet reached the clarity of insight given to the philosophical mind that has passed beyond the necessity for pictorial thinking.

By contrast, Friedrich Schleiermacher (1768–1834) believed the ditch was bridged not in thought but in feeling. He argued by subtle psychological analysis that there is a basic human experience of absolute dependence that indicates that its source is God. The redemptive power of Jesus Christ is in the ability to assimilate the believer into his own perfect God-consciousness, "which was a veritable existence of God in Him."[16] But theologically we are left exploring only the God-consciousness of Jesus or of believers while God remains the mysterious, unconditioned One. It is "the modifications of immediate self-consciousness" that are known but not the reality of God which lies beyond them.

The secular Christologies of the twentieth century bring the myth of the ditch to its final point. In these Christologies it is increasingly apparent that there is no need to cross the ditch because there is nothing on the other side. An absent God is finally equivalent to no God at all. The human side of the ditch is all there is, so we should make the best of it in our "world come of age." A contemporary book on Christology summed up the position in its title, *Jesus for a No-God World*.[17] By the use of linguistic analysis, the Christologies of "the death of God" showed that "God-talk" is not only irrelevant but actually distorts the meaning of Jesus. The importance of Jesus is in the ways he reveals and empowers a new lifestyle for secular existence. The most that can be said is that Jesus is the "stand-in" for an absent God who will appear in the future.[18]

Søren Kierkegaard (1813–55) called all of the Christologies based on the myth of the ditch into question. Yet, paradoxically, he accepted the myth even as he struggled against it. For Kierkegaard, the "ugly broad ditch" had been crossed by the act of God in Christ. However, human beings may come to know this only by a "leap of faith." The disclosure of God in human form violates the basic premise of all thought, namely, that the Infinite cannot become finite without ceasing to be Infinite.[19] When a person responds in faith to this finite disclosure of the Infinite, he or she embraces the "paradox." The only "historical fact" relevant to the "leap of faith" is that once the Eternal became temporal. The truth of this assertion is not dependent upon knowledge of historical events in the life of Jesus. It is known as truth only in the "moment" when the leap of faith is made. Supporting evidence is nowhere to be found except in the passionate subjectivity of the believer. The ditch remains with only the thinnest thread cast across it. There is no coinherence but only an intimation that the ditch is not ultimate. The key symbol is not the coming of light but a leap in the dark. In a strange way, whether in affirming or denying the myth of the ditch, modern Christology has presupposed it, and thought is shaped as decisively by what it denies as by what it affirms.

The Authority of the Myth

The influence of the myth of the ditch does not come from the authority of Lessing or any other modern thinker who has espoused it. Lessing has brought to consciousness the exchange of metaphors from those of coinherence to those of separation. With his myth of the ditch, Lessing expressed an intellectual context that no single philosopher created. This myth has functioned as a funda-

mental picture of the human situation because it expressed a pervasive cultural experience. It is the experience of what contemporary
sociologist Daniel Bell (b. 1919) calls "The Great Profanation."[20]
The ditch symbolizes the alienation of the modern, Western world
from its religious traditions. The ditch is a symbol of the affective,
religious breakdown of Christendom—that great synthesis of Christian faith with Western civilization within which the church has
lived. In part, it is a symbol of protest against distorting religious
traditions in the name of human freedom and autonomy. In part, it
is a symbol of the human rejection of God in self-centeredness. This
duality makes the myth one with which it is difficult to deal. To
reject the myth of the ditch could be the way of opting for a reaction-
ary theology that repudiates all modernity in nostalgic anti-intellec-
tualism. To move beyond the myth could be the opening of a new
possibility for revelation.

It is the prior fact that gave rise
to the myth of the ditch. But at the same time the myth supports and
enlarges this alienation. The myth of the ditch becomes a self-fulfill-
ing prophecy because as a description of the human situation, it
provides the framework by which all data are organized. Starting
with an unbridgeable separation between history and the transcendent, the conclusions are given in the beginning. The best that can be
hoped for is a narrow, tenuous bridge, if any at all, between the
transcendent and the human.

It is impossible to argue away a root metaphor that is pervasive.
A root metaphor is the context of logic and not its product. However, the present state of Christological reflection makes it evident
that the myth of the ditch has become dysfunctional. It no longer
facilitates a creative relationship between the biblical witness to
Jesus Christ and the contemporary spiritual situation. The myth had
a valuable function in the early modern period. It helped clear away
distorting conceptions of Christ and his redemptive work. It opened
the way to modern, critical historical study of the Bible and the
creeds. The emergence of the myth broke the psychic hold of a
defensive Christendom whose traditions were falling into contradiction. But the myth has itself become a new intellectual bondage that
obscures new possibilities for revelation. What is needed now is an

experiment in thought to recapture in contemporary ways the basic metaphor of classical Christology, the metaphor of coinherence.

The exchange of basic metaphors means a reorganization of the data of Scripture, tradition, and human experience. It is what Kierkegaard called "A Project of Thought."[21] The "Project" is neither an inductive nor a deductive argument. It is an attempt to think through a question from a new perspective. What is being proposed here is an experiment which attempts to recapture in contemporary form the metaphor of coinherence. What is proposed is not a reconstruction of patristic Christology or that of scholastic orthodoxy. It is an exercise in contemporary constructive theology utilizing a patristic metaphor.

But how is such an experiment to be verified? The "Project of Thought" being proposed here has deep historical roots. It springs out of a perception of contemporary life in the church. Yet the verifying of this "Project" cannot follow the usual method of historical thought that has dominated modern academic theology. In the historical method, verification of a new theological position comes from establishing its place in an already known and accepted line of doctrinal development. The use of historical verification presupposes a settled context for theological reflection and agreed-upon lines of doctrinal growth. But what is being proposed here is the establishment of a new context for Christological reflection. Instead of following established lines of development, new pathways of thought and belief are being proposed.

A new context for Christological reflection cannot be verified through logical deductions from philosophical systems. While historical and philosophical elements are vital to this "Project of Thought," its verification is basically practical in character. *Does the new context for reflection allow men and women to respond to the self-disclosure of God in Jesus Christ?* This "Project" will be verified if it brings Scripture, tradition, and common human experience into a new relationship in which there is vision and faith. The hope is that a new context for Christology based on the metaphor of coinherence will bring these elements into a new relationship in which there will no longer be conflict but a transparency into the divine life. The dominance of the myth of the ditch over Christological reflection has broken the revelatory relationship between contemporary self-understanding and the witness of Scripture and tradition. This project of thought will be verified if it opens the way for a faithful response to Jesus Christ. To proceed with this project, it is necessary to look more closely at the logic of coinherence.

The Logic of Coinherence

The metaphor of coinherence has been expressed in many ways. Karl Adam (1878–1966) argued that the doctrine of the divine-human *perichoresis* has its foundation in Jesus' logion in the fourth Gospel, "I and the Father are one" (John 10:30).[22] However, the technical theological term only emerges in patristic theology. The earliest use of the term was to characterize the intimacy of the relationship between the persons of the Trinity. It was possible to differentiate Father, Son, and Spirit and yet to maintain the unity of God because they coinhere. The *perichoresis* of Father, Son, and Holy Spirit allows them to be confessed not as three gods but as one God. Gregory of Nazianzus (329–89) used *perichoresis* in his Christology to explicate the relationship between the human and the divine in Jesus. In the defense of the Nicene formula against a lingering Arianism, Gregory sought graphic metaphors to charactize the reality of God's presence in the person of Jesus. His exploration of *perichoresis* helped provide the foundation for the Definition of Chalcedon of Christ existing as "two natures . . . in one person." Because the two natures interpenetrate one another, their union forms the one person Jesus. After the Council of Chalcedon, Maximus the Confessor (c. 580–662) utilized *perichoresis* as the means for interpreting the Definition of the "two natures . . . in one person."[23] But neither Gregory nor Maximus looked upon his use of *perichoresis* as a theological innovation but as a means for explicating what was already well established by the Fathers and councils that preceded them. The term was more fully developed in the traditions of the Eastern church from John of Damascus (c. 675–c. 749) to Gregory Palamas (c. 1296–1359). However, the issues with which these theologians were dealing go back to the earliest beginnings of Christology.

The classical Christology that developed through Nicaea and

Chalcedon has an inner logic that may be summed up in the term *perichoresis*. It affirms the unity of the person of Christ and the distinction of the two natures in such a way that the uniqueness of the natures is preserved and the unity of the person confirmed. No single term can embrace such a complex logic by itself. For this reason, *perichoresis* has sometimes been left untranslated as a technical term in order to protect it from overly simple conclusions about its meaning. It is difficult to find any single word to translate *perichoresis*. It has been translated into English as "pervasion," "interpenetration," "copenetration," "mutual permeation," or "coinherence." The term came over into Latin as *circumincessio* in the twelfth century through a translation by Burgundio of Pisa although the question of *perichoresis* had been approached by Western theologians before this.[24] The word "coinherence" is used as the translation of *perichoresis* to avoid the awkwardness of a transliteration or recourse to a neologism. Yet "coinherence" must be understood as the expression of a comprehensive idea whose logic goes beyond expression by any single term.

The classical Christologies did not invent coinherence as a term to rationalize belief in the incarnation. Rather the reality of incarnation in Jesus was the basis on which the logic of coinherence was developed.[25] Coinherence helped give rational structure to the confession of Christ in "two natures" and "one person." Coinherence was not an idea that already existed in the ancient world, just waiting, as it were, to be applied to the task of interpreting Jesus. Rather, the notion of the divine and human coinherence grew out of what the Christian community had encountered and continued to encounter in the life, death, and resurrection of Jesus. Logically viewed, Christologies cannot be constructed a priori; rather, Christologies are developed a posteriori. Christology is not a logical construction that is brought ready made to resolve the puzzles and problems posed by the appearance of Jesus. The classical tradition in Christology does not first try to establish the possibility of revelation of God and then determine if, in fact, Jesus was that revelation. The classical tradition moves logically from what had happened in Jesus to reflection on how these events reveal God.

Our tendency in formulating Christological questions today is to start out something like this: "In light of what is known of God and about human beings, was Jesus of Nazareth God-human?" The answer to this question given by a person of Christian faith would ostensibly be "yes." The difficulty with this approach is that it presupposes that we know already the truth about God and about humankind. This is a priori thinking. To deal with Christology in this way is to undercut the possibility of revelation in Jesus. To follow this pattern of thought can at most reaffirm what is already known about God.

What is needed is a way of thinking that is open to the genuinely new disclosures in Jesus. Such a pattern of thought would be a posteriori. It starts with the reality of revelation in Jesus and argues in this fashion: "In light of the disclosure of the state of divine-human being in Jesus, what is known about God and humankind?" What is at issue in the Christologies of coinherence is a new definition of God and of human being.

The deity of God and the nature of human being can no longer be defined in isolation from one another. Their definitions must comprehend the intimate relationship between them given in Jesus. Coinherence points to a divinization of the human and a humanization of the divine. But this intimate relationship does not vitiate what is unique about either God or humankind. Jesus Christ is confessed, by the terms of Chalcedon, in two natures "without confusing the two natures, without transmuting one nature into the other, without dividing them into two separate categories, without contrasting them according to area or function. The distinctiveness of each nature is not nullified by the union." God is who God is in the freedom to become human without becoming unlike the divine essence. The deity of God requires no rejection of the human because God has chosen humankind as covenant partner. Conversely, humankind has its full reality in the freedom of union with God and yet does not become unlike its essence.

The logic of coinherence implies that Jesus is not only the revelation of God; Jesus is also the revelation of humankind. Coinherence rejects the division of the events of Jesus' life, death, and resurrection into those related to humanity and those related to divinity. It is not that in frailty, suffering, and death Jesus reveals humanity, while in miracles and resurrection Christ reveals divinity. There has been a tradition of Christian piety that looks at the cross as the disclosure of human existence and at the resurrection as a revelation of God. But coinherence implies that the disclosure in Jesus may be read in the opposite way as well. The death of Jesus is a disclosure of God and resurrection a disclosure of humankind.

One other methodological matter needs attention before undertaking this Christological "Project of Thought." This is clarification of how Scripture is to be used in Christology.[26]

The Use of Scripture

To deal with this problem, it is necessary to investigate just what is implied in confessing the authority of the Bible. First, when a theology claims to be built on the authority of the Bible, it is not affirming a particular kind of historical analysis or critical reconstruction of the text. It is granting authority to the Bible in its canonical form.[27] While critical study has shown that there is a complex literary history behind the present form of the Bible, scriptural authority does not adhere to particular historically discovered levels of tradition. The authority of the Scriptures for the church derives from its unique witness to the Word of God. This authority attaches to the text of the whole Bible as received by the church today. This witness comes from all parts of Scripture, not just those parts identified by historical scholarship as "earlier" or "more authentic." Biblical scholarship has rightly identified a complex development within the texts themselves which is related to the history of revelation. There is, to use the patristic term, a "historical economy" to the history of revelation which is reflected in the biblical texts themselves. But the authority of Scripture inheres in the canonical form of the Bible which the churches confess as authoritative in their statements of faith. As the Bible is used in theology, it cannot be approached as a catalog of discrete and unrelated propositions. Rather, the patterns of meaning in the Bible form the basis for the approach to any particular text. In the words of the Westminster Confession 1.9: "when there is a question about the true and full sense of any Scripture . . . , it must be searched and known by other places that speak more clearly."[28] The appeal to Scripture in theology is to the *sensus plenior*, the fuller sense of Scripture in its canonical form, not to particular texts or traditions isolated by historical analysis.

Second, the authority of Scripture is related to the way in which the church confesses the Bible to be divinely inspired. Conservative Protestantism has tended to make the authority of the Bible dependent upon acceptance of the doctrine of the plenary verbal inspiration of Scripture and the accompanying idea of inerrancy. As modern scientific and historical understanding of the world and of the Bible has rendered this position untenable, it has left the question of what is implied in the confession of the divine inspiration of Scripture unclear. The necessary polemic of both the liberal and neoorthodox theologians has been clearer on what was being rejected than on what was being affirmed about the Bible. Even the classic efforts of Karl Barth (1886–1968) and Emil Brunner (1889–1966) to get around the shibboleth of inerrancy and verbal inspiration have not adequately illumined this problem. The strong turn in contemporary theology to questions of hermeneutics is the inevitable outcome of the confusion over what principles are to guide the interpretation of the Bible when it is being viewed not simply as a religious text from the ancient Near East but as an authoritative witness to the Word of God.

In the new search for an adequate set of interpretive principles undertaken by Paul Ricoeur (b. 1913) and applied theologically by David Tracy (b. 1939), important progress has been made in explicating what is implied when confession is made of belief in the inspiration of Scripture.[29]

The inspiration of Scripture is best understood in light of the question of the referent of the text. To what is it that the text points? Biblical texts have their special function in the life of the church because of the ways in which they point beyond themselves to the revelatory events in the past of which they are a part. To say the Bible is divinely inspired and hence authoritative for the faith and life of the church means that these texts are believed to be a reliable means for identifying and sharing in the revelation of God to which the Bible witnesses. The text in this understanding of inspiration points behind itself to the historical events of revelation. The Bible is a book of *Heilsgeschichte*, and it is itself part of that history of salvation. Historical understanding of the text and the situation out of which it came is basic to retrieving its meaning. The formulation of theology is to be carried out only after the historian has uncovered the real meaning of the text. Without the work of the historical scholar, according to this approach, the theologian is always in danger of lapsing into a mystical, allegorical, or typological exegesis.

Such an interpretive method was typical of neo-orthodoxy or the so-called "biblical theology" movement although in all honesty it must be observed that Barth, Brunner, and the Niebuhrs often exegeted texts with a sovereign freedom that left the biblical historians unhappy. Nonetheless, this tradition was dominated by a hermeneutics of retrieval. The aim was to retrieve the historical revelation to which the text witnesses. In light of such an approach to the Bible, the doctrine of the inspiration of Scripture takes a particular form. To believe in the divine inspiration of Scripture is to believe in the reliability of the biblical text for providing a saving knowledge of revelation. If the referent of the text is behind the text, in the history of salvation, then the inspired Scriptures have authority for Christian faith and life because the Holy Spirit has protected the saving truth within them.

Modern theology has struggled to show how the Bible provides a means for knowing revelation, even as the biblical texts utilize ways of understanding the world and human affairs that have been proved inadequate by scientific and historical knowledge. Such a hermeneutic of recovery is basic for theology, and any attempt to escape its problems by a retreat into anti-intellectual fundamentalism is pointless. There is, however, another way in which to read the doctrine of inspiration.

To confess the inspiration of the Scriptures also means that the referent of the text is in front of the text. To say a text is inspired means that it has a uniquely creative function in the present life of the community of faith because of its ability to point to new revelatory meanings. It is not simply that the Holy Spirit has once inspired the text and left it, like a legal document, to be interpreted by human skill. The inspiration of Scripture means that these texts may be interpreted in relation to contemporary events and persons in the power of the Spirit. To say the referent of the text is in front of the text is to confess belief in the power of the biblical text to be part of an event in which contemporary disclosures of God's saving activity are taking place.

Texts are never merely words isolated from the structures of being out of which they arise. Texts have been articulated out of concrete revelatory events, and now they may function to articulate this revelation in new ways. The inspiration of Scripture means belief in the unique way in which the biblical texts serve as a channel of the self-disclosing activity of God in the present. In this regard, their referent is in front of them in the ever-new human situations to which they may be addressed. They are to be interpreted in light of the questions posed by the contemporary spiritual situation in which they exist, not only from the historical nexus out of which they arose. The hermeneutic of recovery must be supplemented by the hermeneutic of disclosure.

2

The Man Jesus and
the Coming Christ

Historical Jesus—Eschatological Lord

Christological reflection in the modern period has been haunted by two problems. One is how to deal with the human nature of Jesus; the other is what to make of the radical orientation of his message and mission toward the future. Simply calling Jesus a person, albeit a uniquely God-inspired person, was already an option for the humanistic sectarians of the sixteenth century who rejected the classical Christologies. It is an option that has been subject to many variations in liberal and modernist Christologies down to the present.[1] However, for those who sought to affirm the formula of "two natures . . . in one person" the problem of interpreting Jesus' humanity was increasingly acute as modern humanism stressed the integrity and powers of humankind. How could an individual be related to a transcendent God and still be truly human? No matter how difficult this problem, the eschatological character of the message of Jesus and of primitive Christianity was more difficult still. Neither the confessional theologians nor their liberal critics could find release from the problems posed not only by the early church's vision of Jesus as eschatological Lord but by Jesus' own words about the end of this age. Everyone was confronted with the fact that despite the expectation of early Christians, time, like "Old Man River," "just keeps rollin' along." How is it possible to square the religious and moral authority of Jesus with the lack of fulfillment of his promises for the future?

The humanizing in modernity of the imperious Caesar-like Christ of the Byzantine mosaics or the medieval pictures of Jesus as the terrible Judge, while joyously welcomed by religious humanism, has ended with a Jesus incapable of miracles and devoid of majesty.[2] At times, this process has been temporarily halted by the power of church authority or the fervor of evangelical piety. Starting in the nineteenth century, the great mediating theologians, from Isaak Dorner (1809–84) and Gottfried Thomasius (1802–75) to P. T. Forsyth (1848–1921) and Donald Baillie (1887–1954) struggled with psychological insights and philosophical speculation to resolve the problem of the divinity and humanity of Jesus.[3] But the paradox of the divine-human person was not so much resolved as shifted about. Having asked afresh the question of Jesus' humanity, modern theology seemed to be driven by an irresistible logic to affirm nothing but his humanity. What is needed is not so much some higher measure of ingenuity in shuffling about the terms of the problem as a look at the terms in which the problem is formulated. The root of the problem lies in the ways by which what it means to be human is defined. What is needed is a different anthropology than those now being used. What is needed is an anthropology that does not leave humankind isolated within its present potentialities and definitions.

Some modern theologians suggested that the problem of Jesus and eschatology was avoided by the so-called "accommodation theory." Jesus, it was argued, spoke in terms of an immanent, apocalyptic coming of the kingdom of God in accommodation to the first-century worldview. Jesus seemed to have made peace with the fervid religious imagination of his time. His real vision, according to the liberal theologians, was that of a progressive coming of the kingdom through gradual increments of human goodness. The collapse of this historical fiction came with Albert Schweitzer's *Quest of the Historical Jesus* (1906). Schweitzer's analysis of the Gospels left theology faced inescapably with the radically eschatological character of Jesus and the early church. There is no evidence for seeing Jesus as a modern social progressive who talked like a first-century Palestinian. The problem of time had returned with a vengeance to Christology. Schweitzer (1875–1965) himself concluded that no intellectual structures reared in the name of modernity could be integrated into the radical futurity of Jesus' message. The only response he saw was that of personal discipleship devoid of the support of intellectual structures.[4] Eschatology is an inescapable part of Christology. For modernity it is a puzzle that can be neither avoided nor solved.

The questions posed by the humanity of Jesus and the futurity of his message have not been directly related to one another in theological reflection. It would seem the better part of wisdom not to join them and create a compound problem. However, one must bring the humanity and futurity of Jesus together because they are not two unrelated concerns. Rather, time is an essential element in any view of what it means to be human. In fact, relating the question of Jesus' humanity to the radical futurity of his message about the kingdom can provide the basis for a new Christological vision. Simply put, the humanity of Jesus is the new humanity toward which humankind is moving in the future. The New Testament catches this vision in the words of First John, "Beloved, we are God's children now; it does not yet appear what we shall be, but we know that when he appears we shall be like him, for we shall see him as he is" (1 John 3:2). To unfold this vision, it is necessary to see how the definition of human nature is linked to the notion of time.

Human Nature and Time

As Augustine (354–430) observed, the human perception of time is that of a threefold present. There is the present as we experience it, the past as present memory, and the future as present expectation. The recollection we have of the past and the expectation we have for the future are part of the present. The significance of how things were done in the past and the hopes for what will be in the future determine how we act in the present. Human beings struggle to overcome the terrors of history. Our bewilderment about how to act and what to trust is resolved by patterns from the past and visions of the future. This means that the past is never simply over and done, nor is the future an empty repository to be filled by the present. Rather past and future are active dimensions of the present. Over the course of human history, the relative importance of recollection and hope in determining human life has varied. In tradition-directed societies, patterns of life established in the past by the gods and heroes of antiquity are the paradigms for present actions. The future is not vital in determining life for tradition-directed societies because their aim is to live in harmony with the divinely established archetypes already given in the past.

Viewing the future as a factor in the present became possible because the coming of the Christian faith changed the perception of time. What Augustine perceived about time and the flow of human history was grounded in his faith in the kingdom of God given in Jesus Christ.[5] The promise of the kingdom means that history is moving forward to completion instead of in endless cycles of woe and weal. Human life is oriented to a future that is not merely a repetition of the past. The full implications of this changed understanding of time were slow in emerging. Despite the insights of Augustine, the church moved away from the future-oriented visions as Christians accommodated themselves to the tradition-directed societies of the ancient world. This movement is evident in the liturgy. The early Christians prayed earnestly for the return of Jesus (*Maranatha*, 1 Cor. 16:22; Didache 10:6). But by the end of the second century, the prayer had changed to one asking the Lord to tarry until the gospel had been preached to the whole earth.[6] The power of the future luring them forward had waned, and Christians became increasingly at home in the tradition-directed societies of the ancient and medieval world. The sacred structures of church, state, and society dominated life, not the vision of a future kingdom.

In tradition-directed societies, there is no future shock. Well-established patterns of behavior and social organization, sanctioned by religious beliefs, allow the tradition-directed person to handle the threat of an unknown future. For such societies, the traditional patterns of behavior and organization define what it means to be human. The patterns by which such a society lives are summed up in its view of human nature. Two words characterize the vision of human nature in the tradition-directed society: "past" and "above." What it means to be human is defined by what has always been done in the past. The traditional patterns of behavior and social organization define human nature. Philosophically put, this vision is Platonic. What it means to be human is determined by what is above and beyond time, in the ideal realm of the universals. Religiously put, such a society believes that human nature was fixed in creation by God. Human nature is defined by the "past" and determined by the "above"—the transcendent realm of unchanging reality.

The modern view of human nature is marked by two very different terms: "present" and "at hand." Human nature is defined in the modern view by what human beings are capable of doing now. Knowledge of human nature comes from generalizing on the behavior of men and women who are at hand. Knowledge of human nature is a matter of empirical conclusions reached by study of what particular human beings are doing and thinking. Human nature is what we have in common. People no longer believe in the existence of some transcendent reality called "human nature" which determines our being. We are what we are because of our genetic inheritance and our history. All talk of "human nature" is an empirical, statistical generalization of what is common to all men and women.

The limitation of both the tradition-directed and the present-directed views of human nature is that they are unable to deal with a genuinely open future. Tradition-directed societies find human fulfillment in living out the archetypes of human life that are already in existence. Present-oriented societies, like our own, search by empirical means for clues that can guide humankind into the future.[7] Hence the fascination with opinion polling in our society. By statistically identifying current trends, a future is projected that supposedly fulfills the needs and desires now being felt by people. These scientific visions maintain that the human future is determined by trends already at work. The various Marxist schools also claim an empirical, scientific analysis of the means of production that allows the projection of a more fully human future.[8]

But what if the human future is constituted precisely in the ways in which human beings transcend both the past and the present? The uniqueness of human nature lies in its openness to the world and to the future.[9] If genuine novelty exists in the future, it cannot come from the repetition of what now is on a grander or more efficient scale.

A third kind of anthropology is possible beyond the alternative of tradition-directed and present-directed views of humankind. This is a future-oriented anthropology. Such an anthropology proceeds from the assumption that humankind is in a genuine state of becoming that is not limited by past or present. A future-oriented anthropology is not utopian. It is aware that both the promise and the peril of the future come from the ways in which human beings transcend and transform the past to shape the future. Self-conscious intelligence allows human beings to rise above their present situation to envisage new possibilities. We can act upon new options for living. This ability to shape the future may be directed by evil imaginings as well as by visions of human fulfillment. Since this is the case, we need adequate models for the human future. Without such models, we are doomed to live by distorted projections of the past or the present. Without a realistic vision of the future, we are left trapped between nostalgia and wishful thinking.

Beyond Nostalgia and Wishful Thinking

If the full measure of what it means to be human lies in the future, then knowledge of this depends upon a genuine unveiling, a revelation of the human. To project the past or even the present would be distorting. Early Christians saw the impossibility of conceiving human destiny by perceptions of the present. They rejected "the wisdom of this age" and "the rulers of this age" because these forces do not know either the source of the future or the full measure of human destiny. Faith discloses the future, for "no eye has seen, nor ear heard, nor the heart of man conceived, what God has prepared for those who love him" (1 Cor. 2:6–9). The full measure of the human future is part of "a secret and hidden wisdom of God," which "God has revealed to us through the Spirit" (2:10). The people of God know by faith human possibilities unknown to the world. The words to characterize this view of human nature are not "past" and "above," as in tradition-directed societies, nor "present" and "at hand," as in our present-directed society, but "future" and "ahead."

Christian understanding presents a dialectic between what we now are and what we will become. Humankind now has a status through its creation by God and its reconciliation through Christ. As the writer of First John put it, "we are God's children now" (3:2). Yet this status is not stationary. Rather it is the foundation on which a transformation takes place: "it does not yet appear what we shall be." However, there is a disclosure of future possibilities that may be seen in Jesus because "when he appears we shall be like him." At the time of his coming, "we shall see him as he is" and the transformation of humankind will reach its fulfillment. In other words, full human reality lies ahead of us in the kingdom of God. At present, men and women have glimpses of what it means to be fully human. But the full reality of human being is in the eschatological fulfillment by God. Knowledge of the full measure of what it means to be human is not accessible to human reason. It lies in a future beyond our powers to perceive. There must be a revelation of human nature, just as there has to be a revelation of the nature of God. This revelation, Christian faith affirms, has taken place in Jesus Christ.

In a future-oriented anthropology, human nature is not locked within its present potentialities. This allows a definition of salvation in positive terms rather than only negative ones. Salvation is not the infinite extension of life as it now is. Salvation, as characterized by the New Testament, is in the kingdom of God where human existence is translated to a new plane by being freed from the powers of sin and death. The New Testament characterizes salvation in metaphors of transformation. The gospel is not a message of enlightenment that discloses the divine identity humans have already, nor is it a message of liberation from finitude and particularity.[10] The gospel is the good news about the kingdom which is the transformation of the human by God. As Paul says, "not that we would be unclothed, but that we would be further clothed" (2 Cor. 5:4).

This transformation does not come from the infinite extension of human powers of rationality or goodness. The kingdom is a "mystery." It is rooted in God, not in human powers. Paul indicates the scope of this mystery of transformation in First Corinthians: "Lo! I tell you a mystery. We shall not all sleep, but we shall all be changed" (15:51). The human future is not the "sleep" of death. In Christ, human life is not locked within its present potential, existence unto death, but is being freed of sin and death. The kingdom is the fulfillment, not the destruction of the human by the divine. In the present, both the form and power of this kingdom have been given in Jesus and are now at work in the world by the Spirit. We now live by "the first fruits" of the kingdom (Rom. 8:23). An anthropology appropriate to Christian faith has to take into account a future in which human existence is carried beyond what is known in the present. Such an anthropology allows a new reading of much in the New Testament.

Finding Historical Facts

The anthropological assumptions that have driven modern Christology into contradiction are evident in the work of the historians who have investigated the records of the life, death, and resurrection of Jesus. Research into the historical foundations of Christology has proceeded according to the rules of evidence and inference set by modern historiography.[11] This research has brought greater clarity to the historicity of revelation in Jesus than had been reached by the devotional writing of the life of Jesus. But it has posed continuing theological problems that have tempted theologians to limit or replace modern historiography with a method that produces results more compatible with their theological convictions. The struggle with the problem of modern historical understanding continues despite ingenious efforts to solve it.

Historical research into the life of Jesus has been built on the basis of the idea of historical continuity. All our knowledge of the past depends on some assumption of historical continuity. The notion of historical continuity has a common-sense appeal that may be stated simply: what has happened in the past is in continuity with what is happening in the present. The causal relationships observed between events in the present are similar to those that relate events in the past.

In his foundational work on historical method, Ernst Troeltsch argued that the very possibility of historical knowledge is in "the fundamental homogeneity of all historical events." The only way to a knowledge of the past is to investigate it in light of what is going on in human experience now. Historians may seek to enlarge the scope of their experience and expand their empathy for strange and unfamiliar happenings. Yet, in the end, "historical knowledge selects its materials as it may require—and seeks to make it as intelligible as if it were part of our own experience."[12] Knowledge of the past is derived fundamentally by analogy from what is happening in the present. The continuity between the present and the past is the ground for any historical knowledge.

Knowledge of history is obviously not the same as knowledge of the physical world. No exact limits can be drawn around what is or is not a historical event. However, to make history "as intelligible as if it were part of our experience," there are limits to what may be judged "historical." Norms for historicity come from our present understanding of human nature and the world. What has happened in the past is similar to what is happening now. To extend the argument, what may happen in the future is given by what is happening at present.

Fact and Fiction in the Gospels

The impact of this approach to history has been decisive for modern Christology. It meant that in the analysis of the records of Jesus, anything that could not be related to human nature as presently known was rejected as "nonhistorical." Reports of events revealing powers and possibilities that go beyond the present level of human potentialities were rejected as accretions. They were rejected as having never really happened. This approach made necessary a reconceptualization of the miracle stories of the Gospels and the resurrection narratives. When a historical document describes an event that cannot be related to present perceptions of the world, it is not sufficient to declare that it is nonhistorical. A historical explanation of this event must be found to explain its presence in the text. The miracle stories and resurrection narratives are transmuted. The healings, feedings, exorcisms, resurrections, and postresurrection appearances of Jesus are clearly integral to the Gospels. Yet they describe events to which there are few, if any, analogies to be found in contemporary experience. Hence modern historians judge these events to be nonhistorical. But their presence in the texts has to be explained historically. The resurrection narratives illustrate most dramatically how these reinterpretations are made.

The resurrection of Jesus from the dead is, in light of modern historical method, nonhistorical. In human experience, the dead remain dead. Death is an irreversible process in which the delicately balanced homeostasis of human life goes into irreversible disorder. There have been a host of supposedly "historical" explanations of the events that surround the resurrection narratives. There are theories of apparent death, staged either by fraud or by happy coincidence, that allowed Jesus to appear to rise from the dead because he was not really dead at all, only unconscious.[13] More recently, psychological theories have interpreted the resurrection as vivid memory or religious vision. However, contemporary scholarship has forsaken these manifestly unsatisfactory explanations. The resurrection is not open to study in itself, it is argued, but is only historically known through its effects. In itself, it remains the unknown for the historian. Sociologically, it can be studied as the originating event in the life of the church. Existentially, it can be interpreted as the originating event in the coming of the new being given by Jesus.[14]

Similar histories of interpretation can be written for the other miracles of Jesus. The healing miracles have been investigated in light of theories of psychosomatic medicine or Jesus' use of primitive *materia medica.* When such explanations fail to make history "as intelligible as if it were part of our own experience," comparative mythology has been utilized. The presence of the miracle stories is explained by the parallel use of miracle stories in the hellenistic religious texts relating stories of savior gods.[15] Miracle stories are seen in this way as mythological materials used by the early Christians to express their theological convictions about the significance of Jesus. In these schemes of explanation, the locus of the miracle stories is no longer the life of Jesus but the life of the church.

Whenever, in modern debate, theological conservatives raised objections to such interpretations, they were hushed by the warning that their Christologies were really docetic. For if Jesus were fully human, his consciousness, teachings, and works must be those of human life as we know it.[16] To insist upon the historicity of the miracle stories, it was argued, is to introduce a kind of magical spiritualism into Christology that denies the real humanity of Jesus. To maintain the fully human nature of Jesus, is it not necessary to measure the activities of Jesus historically by relating them to common human experience? Hence, when New Testament records point to events that clearly exceed normal human expectations, literary, psychological, or sociological explanations must be utilized to render these accounts consistent with what is considered human. Historically, it is evident that Jesus had an extraordinary impact on people. However, the source of this impact has remained obscure in modern Christology. But to maintain the reality of his humanity, this impact had to come from a life lived within the limits of human nature as it is presently known.

In his critical reshuffling of modern historical method, Wolfhart Pannenberg (b. 1928) points to a way through the historical conjectures that surround the study of Jesus' resurrection.[17] The way out is not through the abandonment of the historical method in the interest of an uncritical reading of the New Testament. The miracles and resurrection of Jesus are historical events and so open to historical research. But this research cannot be fully historical unless it has some way of dealing with truly unique events. While history shows a continuity of events that follows our usual expectations, it also evidences events that break the pattern of normal expectations. Historical study has to be able to deal with new emergents in the course of events. The determination of the scope of the historical by the unswerving application of the notion of the uniformity of human experience and nature excludes, by definition, events in which new human possibilities and powers are discerned. Historical study must stay open to new possibilities for human existence that have emerged in unique events. What follows from this is not the wholesale historicizing of all miracle stories. The theologian and the historian are not left without criteria. As Pannenberg's own work shows, there is a careful task of discernment to be done based on textual evidence and historical inference. What is created is openness to the historicity of events that disclose human powers and possibilities that exceed those known already in present-day experience.

Modern Christologies have held that, while knowledge of God is dependent upon revelation, human nature is known already. Because human nature is known, the scope of the historically possible is also known. Such Christologies have worked on the basis of a present-oriented anthropology that finds the full measure of the human in this present level of human existence. This assumption has blocked historical investigation of what is most vital in understanding the ways in which Jesus reveals new human possibilities. Jesus reveals new human powers and possibilities that are not in direct continuity with present human life, but this does not make these events nonhistorical.

Discerning the Human Future

Revelation of the full scope of human nature is necessary because human life is existence directed toward an end, an eschaton. The structure of human being is directed to an end that has not yet been reached. To use the New Testament words, "it does not yet appear what we shall be" (1 John 3:2). Because of this future-oriented structure of human existence, the true self is obscure now. Our full reality lies in the future. The person who lives by faith is given intimations of this future because he or she shares in the powers of the kingdom. The Spirit is the "guarantee" or "pledge" (Gr. *arrabon*) of the fuller life of the kingdom of God to which the believer is moving (2 Cor. 1:22; 5:5). While the faithful person lives in the midst of sin and death that prevent the complete fulfillment of human nature, he or she has the "first fruits of the Spirit" (Gr. *aparche*) that give hope for the full salvation of the kingdom (Rom. 8:23). But this hope is not for the destruction of creation, nor for the obliteration of the self in the divine infinity. The Christian hope is not for a state of nonattachment, nirvana, nor the absorption of the self in the oversoul. The hope is for the transformation of the self in community. The metaphors of salvation are social—the kingdom or city of God. Ultimate salvation will be when "the creation itself will be set free from its bondage to decay and obtain the glorious liberty of the children of God" (Rom. 8:21). The promised fulfillment is not an existence isolated from the world but is a salvation in, through, and for the world. To make sense of such a promise, our understanding of human nature must comprehend the future form of human existence.

Awareness of the future as a dimension of human life is found not only in Christian theology and has become a factor in contemporary anthropologies as well. There is in contemporary culture a new

awareness of the future as an essential dimension of human existence. The basic conviction of this awareness is that human beings
are not trapped in what Ernst Bloch (b. 1885) has called "a virtually
inexpandable man-as-he-is-at-present existence (*Mensch-Vorhand-
ensein*)."[18] The question for any future-oriented anthropology is
what vision will shape the human future. To say that human nature
is incomplete but is being fulfilled implies some idea of what the new
state of humankind is to be. Such a disclosure of the future would be
possible if the realized person of the future were to have appeared in
history. Such a person would disclose the full measure of human
nature. This appearance is celebrated in the New Testament proclamation of the coming of the kingdom of God in the life, death, and
resurrection of Jesus Christ. Jesus Christ, who appeared in history,
reveals the goal toward which humankind is moving. "It does not yet
appear what we shall be, but we know that when he appears we shall
be like him."

Faith is the means by which a vision of the future is apprehended. Faith arises in the midst of our ignorance of the future—"it
does not yet appear what we shall be." But faith is in the one who
discloses that future—"but we know that when he appears we shall
be like him." Christ is the end before the end so that in knowing
Christ we come to know the fulfilled life of the kingdom of God. This
hope is not in a secular utopia but in a future granted through the
crucified and risen Christ. As Jurgen Moltmann (b. 1926) says, "All
predicates of Christ not only say who he was and is, but imply
statements as to who he will be and what is to be expected from
him."[19]

It is difficult to find an adequate word to express this characteristic of Jesus as "the end before the end." Modern theology has
scouted this question in many ways. P. T. Forsyth perceived the
importance of seeing in Jesus the revelation of the full meaning of
human existence. He saw the necessity of viewing the person of
Christ not only in terms of an act of divine self-emptying, kenosis,
but also in terms of a *plerosis*, the fulfillment of the human.[20] Forsyth
argued that a Christology that dealt only with God's self-limitation
(kenosis) in taking up a fully human life left no room for the fuller
disclosure of human capacities (*plerosis*) that are seen in Jesus. The

Christology that stops with kenosis alone is lopsided because the incarnation did not leave human nature untouched. Incarnation fulfills the human search for the richer, more real life given by God. However, Forsyth did not put his conception of the human *plerosis* in an eschatological context. He used this conception to help make sense out of the historical life of Jesus. However, what is implied by *plerosis* extends from Christ to those who are "in Christ."

Hegel probed the relationship between the disclosure of divine humanity in Jesus Christ and the future. The Christ, when known "in the power of the Spirit," presents the perfection toward which reality is moving as "a Present which is to be conceived of as a Future." The Christ, for Hegel, "is essentially potentiality and means that the last is first and the first last."[21] The Christ is not only a present reality but also the potential of future reality. Yet the key to Hegel's Christology at this point as well as others is in knowing the Christ "in the Spirit."

For Hegel, the term "in the Spirit" does not mean a vision of Jesus given in charismatic experience. Rather "in the Spirit" means knowing Jesus in light of the philosophical notion of Absolute Spirit. The focus is on knowing the idea of God-humanhood that has its real existence in the realm of Absolute Spirit, which is the power of the future. Hegel grasped the future orientation of Jesus but did not relate this to his historical life. He left it purely speculative. In this respect, Hegel stands at the opposite pole from Forsyth.

It is a contemporary theologian, Wolfhart Pannenberg, who brings together the futurity and the historicity of Jesus. Pannenberg links the eschatological significance of Jesus to the concrete details of his life, death, and resurrection. For this purpose he coined the phrase "proleptic eschaton" as a characterization of the resurrection of Jesus.[22] This phrase is a kind of shorthand expression for the link between the historical Jesus and the eschatological faith of the Christian community.

According to its basic dictionary definition, the term "prolepsis" describes a rhetorical device by which a person or event is assigned to a period earlier than the one to which it actually belongs. A prolepsis is the opposite of an anachronism. An anachronism misplaces a person from the past in the present. A prolepsis is the placing of a person of the future in the past or present. In its theological use, Jesus is the prolepsis of the kingdom of God. Jesus is the presence of the end of history who makes the character of the end of history known. The eschaton, the coming of final salvation in the kingdom of God, has not yet fully arrived on the plane of history. Jesus, who has appeared as a historical person, is the disclosure of that eschaton. In knowing Jesus, it is possible to know what the kingdom of God will be like.

When Jesus is known "in the Spirit," there is a disclosure of "the secret and hidden wisdom of God" (1 Cor. 2:7) which is the redemption of humankind in the kingdom. But this wisdom does not come from some suprahistorical vantage point in philosophical reflection or by mystical intuition. The disclosure of God's will of love for the redemption of the world has been revealed in the concrete historical events of the life, death, and resurrection of Jesus. When these events are received by faith as grounded in God, that is, "known in the Spirit," they disclose and empower the future. The vision of the future is to be found Christologically. It is to be exegeted from these events and not arrived at by speculation. To be true to the character of its source in Jesus, this Christological exegesis must begin from below, from the historical events of his life. The paradox confronted by such a way of thinking is in how to relate the particularity of Jesus as a concrete historical person to the universality of the fulfillment promised humanity in the kingdom of God.

Who Does Jesus Save?

The question of how Jesus can be the revelation of a universal destiny for all humankind was treated in the early church theologically by the analysis of the human nature of Jesus. Jesus redeemed all by virtue of having a complete human nature. All aspects of humanity are present in Christ, according to the creeds. The question of inclusivism has taken on new urgency in contemporary theology since the advent of liberation theologies. How can Jesus be the Savior of peoples with whom he has no real identity? Liberation theologies have stressed not some spiritualistic, transcendent salvation granted to the faithful dead in heaven, but a social, political, economic, and psychological liberation that begins here and now. How can Jesus be the source of this salvation for women, Blacks, Native Americans, barrio dwellers in Latin America, and the dispossessed peoples of Asia, Africa, and the Near East? Historically, Jesus was not a woman, a Black, a Native American, nor did he experience the unique forms of exploitation and racism of modern technological societies. How does Jesus become the Savior of peoples whose basic self-definition is alien to his own?

The church has argued that Jesus is Savior because of his identity with humankind in all of its needs and problems. Christ is the High Priest able "to sympathize with our weaknesses, ... who in every respect has been tempted as we are" (Heb. 4:15). All during the controversies leading to the Council of Chalcedon the orthodox teachers argued that Jesus assumed every aspect of human nature. Against all attempts to limit Jesus' identity with the human condition, the patristic theologians said "That [of human nature] which was not assumed could not be saved." This question has come back to Christology with new intensity.

Liberation theologies have attempted to solve this problem by claiming that Jesus can, in fact, be identified with those who seek liberation. Albert Cleage preaches liberation to the oppressed urban Blacks of America in the name of a Black Christ, whom he celebrates along with Mary, a Black Madonna, in a shrine at Cleage's church in Detroit. The piety of the Black church has long centered around a Christ figure who shares in the sufferings of these people. Liberation theology has addressed the oppressed peoples of Latin America who picture Jesus identified with their sufferings in the folk art of their crucifixes. The Jesus who walks the way of sorrow with them is the one through whom comfort is given in the present and promise of liberation is found for the future. Yet there are severe difficulties to basing any claim for salvation on Jesus' *historical* identity with particular groups.

Wide-ranging historical speculations have sought to establish the identity of Jesus with a variety of groups seeking salvation. Speculations over the possibility that Jesus was androgynous have hoped to establish Christ's identity with people of both sexes seeking salvation. Attempts have been made to prove that Jesus was married so he

can bring saving insight to floundering marriages. Others have
sought to picture Jesus as homosexual, so he can bring liberation to
those who are oppressed by a homophobic society. The difficulty
with all of these speculations is that they lack historical grounding.
The historical evidence is that Jesus was a first-century Jewish male
who lived within the value system and worldview of his time and
place. The reality of his humanity means that he lived within the
forms of self-consciousness shared by his contemporaries.

For theologians concerned with Jesus as the deliverer from
social, political, economic, and cultural oppression of the Black,
Latino, and other colonialized peoples, the identification between
these peoples and Jesus can be directly established. Historically, it is
clear that Jesus lived as a member of an oppressed race, exploited by
a colonialist empire, and that he went to his death at the hands of a
corrupt government and religious establishment. So in *A Black Theology of Liberation,* James Cone can say, "the *literal* color of Jesus is
irrelevant."[23] Jesus is "black" in the sense that he is completely identified with the oppression and exploitation that has characterized
Black existence in our racist society. Through this identity, Jesus
reveals what is central to the liberation theology, *"God himself is
present in all dimensions of human liberation."*[24] Jesus is the prototype
of the martyr-savior figure of the movements for political and economic freedom the world over. Christ is identified in the liberation
movements as the deliverer because he, like all oppressed people,
was the victim of social, economic, political, and psychological
exploitation that finally "lynched" him on the cross. The death
squads of El Salvador, the night riders of the Klan, and the security
police of South Africa play the role of the Roman soldiers. Jesus is
the Savior for oppressed people because he has shared their common
oppression and triumphed to bring the good news of liberation into
the new life of the kingdom of God.

However, the problem of identification with Jesus in relation to
the movement for the liberation of women is intractable. Jesus was a
male who lived in an ancient society whose ethical and religious
systems were characterized by male domination. While Jesus is a
symbol of liberation, is he a means of the liberation of women or
only of men? The reply that has been made to this question from the

standpoint of traditional theologies is that Jesus is the Savior of all humankind from sin and death. Women and men share together in their bondage to sin and death, and hence both are delivered by him. But there is a persistent problem with this answer as has been shown by Mary Daly (b. 1928) and Rosemary Radford Ruether (b. 1936).[25] The church, the institution that supposedly arose as a result of the salvation brought by Jesus, has been persistently characterized by male domination. While Jesus delivers from sin, his ability to deliver the church from the sins of sexism has been limited, to say the least. Some of the feminist critics have concluded that this is a problem that cannot be remedied by ethical reform and organizational rearrangements in the church. The situation is hopeless, as Mary Daly concluded, because the underlying religious symbol system of church and Bible are irremediably male-centered. The attempts to deal with these criticisms depend upon being able to identify elements in the ministry of Jesus and the history of Christianity that are free of an ideology of male domination.

The fact that the church very early in its history took over the male-dominated patterns of ancient Judaism and Greco-Roman antiquity, as it was later to take over attitudes of social, economic, and political domination, cannot be denied. Krister Stendahl (b. 1921) proposed an argument in favor of a nonsexist Christianity.[26] He argued that there is, even in the New Testament, a distinction between law and gospel. The rules and regulations by which the earliest Christians regulated their lives is law. It is, as is all law, a reflection of the cultural accommodations and sinful self-interest that distorts all law, even that given by God. Law is not the basis of the church nor the norm for its life. This basis can only be the gospel. The gospel is summarized by an inclusiveness and egalitarianism that overcomes all systems of domination set by law. "For as many of you as were baptized into Christ have put on Christ. There is neither Jew nor Greek, there is neither slave nor free, there is neither male nor female, for you are all one in Christ Jesus" (Gal. 3:27–28). The gospel is the basis of the church, and it sets the future of the church. But this does not mean that the church is able to live perfectly out of the gospel. The church is the community of the forgiven, not the perfect. The full implications of this verse were not fully realized even by the person who wrote it, as a study of Paul's letters shows, but it still remains the foundation of the church.

Such a line of reasoning marks an important start on the question of overcoming sexist and racist interpretations of Scripture, but the question remains: is there evidence of a different pattern at work in the earliest Christian community than the one that was later to arise in the church? In her "Feminist Theological Reconstruction of Christian Origins," Elisabeth Schüssler Fiorenza (b. 1938) reexamines the critical transition in the history of Christianity when the church emerges as an organized religious community from the immediate context of Jesus and his ministry.[27] She identifies two major theological concepts for understanding Jesus that stand outside the sexist and racist tendencies that have affected later Christian theology and church life. These are Jesus' teachings on the kingdom of God, which express the dynamic of what she calls "the Jesus movement," and the gift of the Holy Spirit, which is the source of the new creation, which is the dynamic of "the missionary movement" that carries the gospel into the world. Kingdom and Spirit provide the means by which Christological reflection may be guided to conclusions that reach beyond the sexist patterns of traditional theology.[28] It is only as the kingdom loses its eschatological character and is converted into a metaphor for the church as a social, political, religious institution that the concept "kingdom" assumes its patriarchal, exploitative patterns. Similarly, it is only as the charismatic power of the Spirit movement threatens the order and progress of the church into the world that the Spirit becomes controlled by the sacramental powers of a male priesthood. The possibility of moving beyond sexism and racism lies in rethinking the kingdom in the power of the Spirit.

Our "Project in Thought" has to encompass the possibility of becoming part of a new history of interpretation that moves along different lines than those by which the concepts of "kingdom" and "Spirit" have been interpreted before. Our task will be to see how the person of Jesus is related to the kingdom of God, for it is the kingdom that is the universalizing concept by which the earliest Christians illumined their faith in Jesus.

3

Jesus and the Kingdom of God

The Particular and the Universal

Jesus lived in first-century Palestine as a Jew. The religious traditions, political realities, and socio-economic conditions of that time shaped his life. His teachings reflect the rabbinic traditions of his day; his hopes for the future draw on the apocalyptic visionaries of the time; Roman political power set limits to his existence and finally claimed his life. He was a person of his time and place. All too often, Christian piety and theology have blurred this fact by dissolving his historical particularity in the overarching claims made for his universal importance. The classical tradition in Christology carefully insisted on the completeness of his human nature against all Gnosticism. But the patristic Christologies were unable to hold this conviction up to a fully historical analysis of his particularity. By contrast, modern Christologies have been deeply concerned with the "Jesus of history." But these Christologies have difficulty in identifying the universal elements in this "Jesus of history."

As knowledge of the historical setting of Jesus and his ministry increased, the gap between his modes of self- and world-understanding and ours deepened. At first, historicism held out the promise of bringing us from behind dogmatic abstractions to a real human Jesus in whom we could believe. But the promise was illusory. Instead, historicism has left us with the strange figure of Jesus, the apocalyptic teacher, itinerant preacher or magician, who remains a possible object of faith only because so little is known about him. As Gerhard Ebeling (b. 1912) put it, "Jesus is constitutive for Christology."[1] This is not a truism. It is a fundamental point of departure which has too often been pushed aside.

The importance of Jesus as historically known for theology was given creedal formulation in a contemporary confessional statement in the Reformed tradition. The "Confession of 1967" of the Presbyterian Church, U.S.A., gives priority in its Christological sections to the historical particularity of Jesus. "Jesus, a Palestinian Jew, lived among his own people and shared their needs, temptations, joys, and sorrows." However, the Confession goes on to claim, "In Jesus of Nazareth true humanity was realized once and for all" (I.A1). How is it possible to claim that this one, particular, historically conditioned life was the realization "once and for all" of true humanity? The answer lies in how Jesus is related to the kingdom of God.

Jesus is the disclosure of true humanity. Yet for Christian faith he is more. Jesus is the power by which all of humankind is moved toward the human fulfillment he revealed.[2] Jesus reveals human destiny through a unique relationship to the kingdom of God. By tracing the logic of what the New Testament says about the kingdom of God, the universal importance of Jesus will become clear. What the New Testament teaches about the kingdom fits no simple pattern. The kingdom is universal in scope because it is the righteous reign or rule of God over all. It is realized when men and women are obedient to the will of God. But this obedience is not the source of the kingdom. The Lord God is the source. Social, political, and economic life may be transformed by the presence of the kingdom, but they do not create it. The natural order and its evolutionary processes may be transmuted by the coming of the kingdom, but these processes do not constitute the kingdom. Central to the teachings about the kingdom by Jesus and the early church is the priority of the action of God the Lord. Because it is the kingdom of the one and only God, it is a universal reign of righteousness. This means that while the kingdom comes to expression in a particular time and place through a particular person, its power may appear in all places.

The history of traditions in the New Testament shows how elements of Jewish eschatology were brought into a new configuration by being related to Jesus. The historical details of this reinterpretation are complex. It is theologically clear that the kingdom functions as the means for relating the Lordship of God to the existence of Jesus and his followers. The kingdom is not a verbal sign applied to

Jesus to give him meaning. The kingdom of God is the power of new being that enters the world through Jesus. The life, death, and resurrection of Jesus discloses both the pattern and power of God's redemptive activity in all reality because the kingdom is universal. The response to Jesus, his teachings, and his mighty acts is a response to the kingdom of God (John 8:38; Luke 9:26). But what is it that makes such a relationship between Jesus and the kingdom possible?

Time and the Kingdom of God

The New Testament makes three related affirmations about the kingdom of God.

First, in the life, death, and resurrection of Jesus Christ, the promise of the kingdom made through the prophets has been fulfilled. His ministry, crucifixion, and resurrection are the saving events by which the kingdom is established.

Second, through Jesus' resurrection and the gift of the Spirit, men and women may now start to share in the kingdom. The kingdom is present, "in the midst of" or "within" those now alive (Luke 17:21). The disciples of Jesus have not yet entered into its full reality, but they have the Spirit as the "guarantee" (2 Cor. 1:22; 5:5) or "first fruits" (Rom. 8:23) of the full redemption given in the kingdom.

Third, the full disclosure of the kingdom will be given with the coming of Jesus as Lord at the end of history. The future actualization of the kingdom will bring an end to the "wars and rumors of wars" that characterize life as we now know it.

The reality of the kingdom is the same in all three cases: past—in and through the ministry of Jesus; present—through the "first fruits of the Spirit"; and future—in consummation. Its power of new being is that of God the Lord who transcends time yet is free to enter all times.

The kingdom appears in time but is not bound by time, so Jesus spoke of the immanence of the kingdom. It is "at hand" (Mark 1:15). He also spoke of the presence of the kingdom "in the midst of you" (Luke 17:21). It is present now like a banquet spread out on a table to which the guests are called (Matt. 22:1–10; Luke 14:15–24). Yet, while the kingdom is present, it is also growing to ever greater reality (Mark 4:26–29). Its power was to be seen in Jesus' driving out demons while still in the present age (Luke 11:20). Yet the kingdom is also compared to a future crisis that will break in at the end of history in judgment (Matt. 25:1–46).

These different ways of talking about the kingdom of God are conflicting when related to our common-sense conception of time. If the past is sealed off from the present, only to be recalled by memory or historical reconstruction, and the future is an empty receptacle to be filled with the hopes and fears of the present, then the New Testament teachings about the kingdom fall into contradiction. The modern scholarly argument over "realized" versus "purely futuristic" eschatologies in the New Testament comes to an impasse because of such an inadequate conception of time. However, contemporary physics and evolutionary theory have developed other ways of conceptualizing time that can comprehend the complexity of the biblical pictures of the kingdom.

The movement through time may be helpfully measured as clock time in certain circumstances. But clock time does not encompass fully the nature of time. It is at best an abstract measure of time. Time is not uniform and linear. Time is capable of being stored or compressed.[3] So it is possible to conceptualize the "time-binding" or "time-bridging" aspects of the kingdom of God. The power of the future, the kingdom of God, that emerged in the past, is available in the present. The kingdom may be said to store time because the redemptive power of the historical Jesus, his life, death, and resurrection, is presently available. That "Great Time"—the time of redemption—enters our time.

The kingdom may also be said to create new time because its powers create new possibilities for the future. Humankind is not limited to its present set of spatio-temporal relationships. New configurations of time and space open the possibilities for existence that are not determined by options already known. The freedom of God as Creator means God is not limited to the rigid causalities as conceived by the Newtonian-Euclidean worldview. In divine creative and redemptive activity, God has the freedom to create new configurations of space and time in which space and time are no longer barriers blocking us off from one another. The kingdom of God is the biblical expression for this freedom of God to intersect human existence at all points—past, present, and future. Hence, in light of the power of the kingdom, it is appropriate to speak of the presence of the past. The redemptive power of the past acts of the historical Jesus is not isolated in the past only to be reconstructed by historical research but is actually present as the source of forgiveness and new life now. The faithful exist "in Christ" and so share his death and resurrection of the power of new being right now (Gal. 2:20; Rom. 6:1–11). Paul gives the most unequivocal expression to this linking of present existence to the historically given reality of Jesus in his affirmation, "for to me to live is Christ" (Phil. 1:21).

The full redemption that will be actualized in the future already exists and may be entered now through the power of the Spirit. Deeds done now in response to the will of God are deeds of the kingdom. The giving of "even a cup of cold water" (Matt. 10:42) is not a transitory act because it is an act of the kingdom, so Jesus said of the disciple who gives it, "he shall not lose his reward." Our present existence has power to build the future despite the apparent destruction of human goodness by the passage of time.

The Kingdom and the Response to Jesus

In the words and deeds of his ministry, Jesus appeared as the herald of the kingdom. He proclaimed the kingdom and called for a response to its presence as revealed in what he did and said. The response people make to Jesus and his call to discipleship is a response to the kingdom. To reject Jesus and his words in this present evil age is to be rejected by God in the judgment at the final coming of the kingdom (Matt. 16:27; Mark 8:38; Luke 9:26). The kingdom is coming as divine judgment on the powers that control this present age. But those who would be Jesus' disciples must have faith to discern the kingdom in the present when the evidences of divine sovereignty are perilously sketchy and ambiguous. To be sure, in Jesus' words and deeds there were limited but authentic disclosures of the kingdom and its power. Early confessional statements remember Jesus as the one "attested to you by God with mighty works and wonders and signs (Acts 2:22; Luke 24:19), yet faith was needed for these works to take place (Matt. 13:58; Mark 6:5–6). Similarly in Christ's preaching about the Son of Man or the Messiah who would be God's agent in bringing in the kingdom, Jesus gave no clarity as to his identity with this one. While he spoke and acted "as one who had authority" (Mark 1:22), his identity was veiled in what Søren Kierkegaard called "the profoundest incognito. . . . almightily maintained."[4] Having taken "the form of a servant" (Phil. 2:5–8), the secret of his identity with the one who brings in the kingdom is only disclosed to the disciple who lives by faith and obedience (John 7:16–17).

In the emerging Christology of the church, the obscurity of the relationship between Jesus and the one who brings in the kingdom is overcome. The kingdom is "the kingdom of Christ and of God" (Eph. 5:5). Its coming will be the end of history and the appearing of Jesus as the exalted Son of Man. It will be "his appearing and his kingdom" (2 Tim. 4:1). The proclamation of Jesus and of the kingdom becomes identified (Acts 28:31). The coinherence of Jesus with the kingdom of God received confirmation in his death and resurrection because these are the eschatological events of triumph over sin and death that establish the kingdom on earth. As Karl Barth put it, "Jesus Christ is Himself the established kingdom of God."[5] Through these events, the identity of Jesus with the power of the kingdom is revealed. But this was more than a verbal clarification.

The resurrection-exaltation of Jesus is not merely a shift in the structure of identity but in the structure of being. The death and resurrection of Jesus are his exaltation to a new and higher status in which he becomes "both Lord and Christ" (Acts 2:36; Phil. 2:9–11). The exaltation of Jesus is a change in the being of God. It is not simply human history that is divided by Jesus into B.C. and A.D.; the history of God is also divided in this way.

In the preaching of the church, the language about the kingdom undergoes further transition. The use of the term kingdom of God decreases, and in its place are found other ways to describe the new being in Christ. The new social reality created by the reconciling work of Christ is a "New Person" in which the previously divided races of Jew and gentile have been united (Eph. 2:15). A single body has been formed with Christ as its head (Col. 1:18). This body is a corporate reality in which members share, each contributing his or her own unique part. When considered as a whole, it is the Body of Christ. The transition from language about the kingdom to language about communal life "in Christ," as part of the new humanity, or Christ's Body, is made possible by the resurrection-ascension. Because he has now been exalted in the Godhead, Jesus is no longer merely the herald of the kingdom. The divine-human coinherence as the power of new life in the kingdom has been established by him. What is awaited is the final realization of the kingdom in human affairs.

The relationship of Jesus to the kingdom implies both a realized and a futuristic eschatology because Christ has the divine power to bridge time. It is realized because the power of the kingdom is now in existence and available to men and women. Jesus' life, death, and resurrection provide all the salvation that will ever be needed. It does not have to be repeated (Heb. 9:25–28). Jesus is not one of a series of divine appearance forms that disclose God at various critical points in human history. He was not an avatar or bodhisattva who needed to appear again and again to remind humankind of the eternality of God or the moral law. His life, death, and resurrection are epochal.[6] Those who live now in the interim between the granting of salvation and its fulfillment are grafted into the Body of Christ and live by hope through sharing the being of the kingdom. There is hope for the future because Jesus has the divine power to create new time.

The experience of new life in Christ points in two directions: it points backward to its source in Jesus Christ, and it points forward to its fulfillment in the future. However, neither future hope nor past remembrance drains the present of its meaning because Jesus gives power to live faithfully amid the terrors of history. The faithful person may be confident in hope because of what has already been revealed in Jesus. The life, death, and resurrection of Jesus Christ provide a historically given foundation for hope (1 Cor. 15:17–21). The reality of the kingdom is not that of a fantasy or a wish projection. It has a basis that is open to historical investigation. It is revealed in the life, death, and resurrection of Jesus.

Present participation in the kingdom through the power of the

Spirit is the ground of confidence for those who seek to be faithful in this "present evil age" (Gal. 1:4). This participation is only fragmentary and imperfect. Now the faithful live by the "first fruits" or "guarantee" of the kingdom in the charismatic power of the life of faith. But this fragmentary sharing in the new being of the kingdom is real. It is based on the being of God himself. This Christian hope is disclosed in two ways. The historical Jesus provides an objective, empirical foundation to this hope, and the work of the Spirit offers a subjective, personal foundation for it.

Present and Future

The vision of human fulfillment given by Christian faith stands in contrast to other models for conceiving the human future. Despite the seemingly irresistible temptation of Christians to equate the kingdom with social powers, political, and economic movements, both sacred and profane, the New Testament does not teach that the kingdom is to emerge from forces already at work in human history.[7] It would be more accurate to say that the kingdom exists already and is drawing history toward itself. The difficulties of describing this vision of the future are great because there is no ready-made conceptual framework to deal with the time-binding quality of the kingdom.

Pierre Teilhard de Chardin (1881–1955) struggled with only partial success to provide such a conceptual scheme. His efforts were plagued by neologisms that lacked precise definition, and his evolutionary theory ran aground on contemporary developments in that theory. Yet his poetic vision caught a crucial dimension of any theology of the kingdom. For Teilhard, Jesus is both the disclosure of the future and the power that allows the universe to move toward that future. The concrete historical reality of Jesus has been given cosmic significance through the resurrection-ascension. As risen Lord, Jesus Christ becomes the "Omega Point" toward which history is moving.

The Omega Point is more than the individual being of Jesus as a historical person. It is the transformed human community of those existing "in Christ."[8] The Omega Point may also be conceived as the goal toward which evolutionary process is moving. However, the evolutionary process itself is not the guarantee of reaching the Omega Point. The evolutionary process has itself led down many dead-end streets. Evolutionary process is now operating not only out of its own patterns but also is being shaped by human decisions. So the process can fall into self-contradiction and chaos.[9] The world process needs redemption, not just time for fulfillment. The redemptive work of Christ as Omega Point is to provide both the pattern of new being and spiritual empowerment for human history to move toward completion. Christ has this capacity because the end of history is already complete and present in him. For Teilhard, it is not that the Omega Point, or kingdom of God, is emerging from the vitalities of history. Christ is "the Prime Mover Ahead," who as risen Lord, is drawing the world toward fulfillment.[10]

Wolfhart Pannenberg, working out of a different model for the future, deals apologetically with the modern objections brought against the Christian doctrine of hope. If the only reality that the kingdom has now is that of an intense wish for a better future or as a program of ethical aims, then all talk of the kingdom may be dismissed as a mere human wish or speculation. Sociological or psychological explanations may be advanced, as they have been by Marxist and Freudian critics, to explain how the Christian vision of the future emerges as the wish projection of oppressed people. Against this objection, Pannenberg insists that the kingdom of God is "ontologically grounded in itself."[11] The kingdom already exists in its own right. The kingdom is not a wish or speculation. If that were the only reality the kingdom had, it would soon be betrayed into the indifferent acceptance of the status quo or become a program of anarchic hysteria or religious fanaticism. The hope for the kingdom is a hope that may be held with confidence, so the faithful person can "wait for it with patience" (Rom. 8:25). The kingdom has a reality of its own not created by the intensity of human beliefs or desires because it is grounded in what God has done through Jesus. The warrant for such hope is historically given in the life, death, and resurrection of Jesus. This warrant is tied to the historicity of Jesus and, more particularly, the historicity of the resurrection.

Talk about the end of history is not speculative for Christian faith because the end is anticipated in the new life given by the Holy

Spirit. This present sharing in the kingdom means that the church is given certain charismata, gifts of grace, by which it realizes the future in the present. Human renewal, forgiveness, and healing are expressions of the future of the kingdom in the present that are granted by the Spirit. The church lives now by the "first fruits" of that greater reality of the kingdom which is to come. In this faith, the believer is delivered from utopian perfectionism about the church. It is not equal to the kingdom. Its failures and faults do not imperil the kingdom. But the faithful also escape nihilistic despair about the church because the kingdom is present in it, its preaching, sacraments, and fellowship. The presence of the kingdom is fragmentary but real.

The link by which the faithful presently share in the kingdom may dwindle into insignificance before the tragedies of life. The promise of the kingdom may be overwhelmed by the terrors of history. This is why Jesus warns about the danger of losing faith. So terrible is the onslaught on faith that even "the elect" are in danger of falling into unbelief. In a world of overwhelming evil, perseverance becomes the cardinal virtue (Mark 13:20–22). To be faithful means to live in the interim "as if" human life is redeemable.

Freedom—Human and Divine

The assertion that the kingdom is already established in Jesus Christ raises difficult questions about human freedom. Does not the assertion that the end of history is already given in Jesus make it impossible to speak of the world, or any individual within it, as having an open future? Or looked at in another way, does not the conviction of the certainty of the coming of the kingdom undercut the seriousness of ethical decisions and religious choices? How is it possible to make sense out of the Gospel imperatives to repentance, faith, and obedience, in a world shaped by the sovereign will of God, and in no way dependent on human choices? The traditional arguments between Augustinians and Pelagians or Calvinists with Arminians wrestle with these issues. But the traditional formulations flounder because they operate on the basis of an inadequate conception of time.

In the interim between the disclosure of the kingdom and its full realization, rejection of new being in Christ is a possibility. Such rejection is an obstruction of the will of God in the world. God does not will the rejection of life in the kingdom that people can and do make. The Lordship of God over the kingdom does not mean that, at any given moment, all events in the world are God's will. To say that God's intention of love for the fulfillment of the world is fulfilled in Jesus does not mean that all of the events leading to the kingdom have been fully determined already. The Lordship of God lies in the divine power to redeem the tragic consequences of human disobedience and faithlessness. There is an interaction between the divine freedom to love and human freedom to accept or reject that love. But this interaction is of such a sort that human freedom does not vitiate God's freedom to fulfill the divine will of love in the kingdom, and, conversely, the freedom of God does not destroy human freedom.

Traditional Augustinian-Calvinistic theologies built upon an abstract notion of God's sovereignty insist that the only guarantee of the Christian hope is in the complete control of all events by God. If God does not control everything now, there is no certainty of God's being able to bring in the kingdom. Good events are God's blessing on faithfulness and obedience to divine will, while suffering, death and tragedy are divine judgment upon sin and disobedience. In such theologies, to grant high importance to human choices would be to undercut the divine sovereignty and, hence, God's ability to bring history to completion in the kingdom.

The movement through human history, in this model of God's sovereignty, may be likened to an audience viewing a movie. The movie is complete from the very first moment it is shown. Not only is the conclusion certain; all the actions leading to the conclusion are fully determined. The audience may have strong emotions about what they see. They have the freedom to like or dislike what they see. However, neither their emotions nor their preferences in any way affect the course of the film or its outcome.

Such a scenario for the future is supported not only by its logical neatness but also by deeply religious motives. While there is often a terrifying mystery to God's will, there is immense confidence in knowing that nothing is outside the will of God, be it negative or positive. A long and vital tradition of Christian piety has sought orientation amid the terrors of history by including the negative as judgment and the positive aspects of human life as redemption, both stemming from the direct will of God.

However, the logical neatness of this model is endangered by the impossibility of making God the source of evil. Evil cannot be reduced to expressions of God's righteous judgment on sin. There is a wild irrationality about evil. The Westminster divines wisely added to their assertion of God's ordination of "whatsoever comes to pass" the reminder that in no way is God "the author of sin, nor is violence offered to the will of the creatures" (3.1).[12] Logical consistency is here sacrificed to preserve the ethical integrity of the biblical vision of God's relation to the world.

What is necessary to express the biblical vision of God's relation to history is a conceptual model built on personalistic lines rather than through an abstract logical analysis of the notion of absolute sovereignty. Jesus' parables of the kingdom probe in personal terms the limits of human freedom and divine freedom as they impinge on one another.

The parables of the prodigal son, the lost sheep, and the lost coin illumine the dialectic between God's freedom to love and human freedom in responding to that love. In the parable of the prodigal son, the focus is on the return of the son to the waiting father. The prodigal rejected the will of his father and broke fellowship with him. The father was left waiting until the son "came to himself" (Luke 15:17). The power of the father to give the son new being is real, even as the son suffers the consequences of his misused freedom "in a far country." The son returns, not because of the coercive power of the father, but in an act of freedom. The power or willingness of the father to receive and renew the son is never called into question. The father goes out to meet him and imposes no conditions on his loving forgiveness. Yet the son was left to live with the consequences of his rejection of the father until he was ready to come into a new relationship with him. The father was not indifferent to the decisions of his son. But the father's power to love and transform his son was not diminished by the son's rejection.

Similarly, in the parables of the lost coin and the lost sheep, the focus is on the joy when the lost are found (Luke 15:3–10). The sovereignty of God does not mean indifference to human decisions or the accidents of history. Whether lostness is an outcome of a conscious misuse of freedom or the result of human carelessness or sheer contingency, God is concerned with finding the lost. There is to be "joy in heaven" at the return of the lost. God is Redeemer, not by the denial of freedom or even contingency, but by divine power to overcome their consequences. God has, as it were, a commitment to human freedom. Human freedom before the power of the kingdom is real and leaves, as S. N. Bulgakov (1871–1944) put it, room "for a certain risk of unsuccess."[13] Only when the divine work of love is complete and God is "all in all" (1 Cor. 15:28, KJV) will the divine commitment to human freedom be at an end.

The reciprocity between the kingdom of God and human decisions and intentions must be stated carefully. Initially, it can only be stated negatively. The destructiveness that comes from rejection of the kingdom does not destroy the power of the kingdom. The warrant for this assertion is the death and resurrection of Jesus. In his death, Jesus, the just one who lived by the will of God, is the victim of the destructiveness loose in human history. Jesus, the "man attested to you by God," was "crucified and killed by the hands of lawless men" (Acts 2:22–23). The death of this one sent by God is the assault of evil on the kingdom. Christ's resurrection is the vindication of the one who trusted fully in God. Jesus' resurrection reveals the limits of death. The power of death is not the final measure of life in this world. Resurrection means the final destructiveness—death itself—is not outside the power of God to give life. The destructiveness let loose by sin cannot overwhelm God's power to realize the kingdom although its tragic consequences are terrifyingly real.

The power of the kingdom transcends the force of human decisions by being able to redeem their tragic consequences. The New Testament has a dialectic between assertions of victory over death and the continuing power of death. All things are "put in subjection" to Christ including death itself. Yet Christ "must reign until he has put all his enemies under his feet. The last enemy to be destroyed is death" (1 Cor. 15:25–27). In the Epistle to the Hebrews, the vision of the crucified and risen one is the guarantee during this time of uncertainty of the victory of God over sin and death. Now "we do not yet see everything in subjection to him" (i.e., to humankind). The chaos and contradictions of life are all too real. "But we see Jesus, who for a little while was made lower than the angels, crowned with glory and honor because of the suffering of death" (Heb. 2:8–9).

As long as men and women live in the interim between the revelation of the kingdom and its consummation, they live in the face of death. However, since the appearance of the powers of new being in the kingdom, death is no longer final but the way to resurrection. The power to transform the negativity of death exists and may be shared, in a fragmentary way, now by faith. Entrance to the new being of the kingdom is through participation in the death and resurrection of Christ (Rom. 6:3–11; Gal. 2:20). Resurrection presupposes death; it does not exist, as it were, by itself. Death is necessary to it. So, the faithful people are called upon to live both "under the cross" and "in light of the resurrection."

To share by faith in the death and resurrection of Christ is to have the freedom to live creatively amid the tragedies of this age because one recognizes them not as "death throes" but as "birth pangs." The emergence of the kingdom is possible only in the convulsive leap of death and resurrection. The cross has the power to create new persons because in it death is revealed not as "a dead-end street" but the precondition of resurrection. The "old being" must die. The "old order" must pass away. Viewed from the vantage point of this world these acts of dying seem only void and empty. What the cross shows is that the passing of the present is the ground of a new future. In light of the cross and resurrection of Christ a new perspective is given on death. As Teilhard says, "What was by nature empty and void, a return to bits and pieces, can, in any human existence, become fullness and unity in God." So it is that finally, "the Christian is not asked to swoon in the shadow, but to climb in the light, of the Cross."[14]

4

The Death of Jesus
as the Disclosure of God

Atonement Doctrine and the Death of Jesus

Paul insisted upon the centrality of the death of Jesus for Christian faith. "For I decided to know nothing among you except Jesus Christ and him crucified" (1 Cor. 2:2). The question is just how a death can be the key event in salvation history. Death is the enemy. Yet, from its earliest levels, Christian tradition has claimed a saving importance for Jesus' death. Many images have been used to unlock the mysterious connection between death and salvation. Christ's death is called the sacrifice of a lamb, a shepherd's life given for his sheep, a ransom of a slave, the payment of a debt, atonement by a priest, the vicarious satisfaction of a legal penalty, or the victory over the demonic powers.[1] No one of these images emerges as supreme in the New Testament, the patristic writers, or the early councils. Unlike the deliberations on the person of Christ, which led to the decisions of Nicaea and Chalcedon, the work of Christ was given no single dogmatic formulation by the early councils. Instead, these images coexist as witnesses to the saving mystery of Jesus' death on the cross.

Not until the end of the eleventh century in Anselm's *Cur Deus Homo* did systematic atonement doctrine start to emerge. Systematic theologians selected one of the scriptural or traditional images of Jesus' death and made it the central one around which all others were to be interpreted. The development of atonement doctrines has unfolded as one image has replaced another as the central one for disclosing the saving importance of Jesus' death. While this method held the promise of systematic order, it has deflected attention from the historical context of his death. These traditional doctrines of atonement have reached an impasse that cannot be resolved by adjudicating the relative historical priority, dogmatic authority, or moral superiority of one image of the death of Jesus over the others.[2] The fundamental need is to look historically at the meaning of Jesus' death. The immediate context for understanding his death is the crisis of faith it created for Jesus and his earliest followers.

Jesus and his earliest followers lived by faith in God as given religious form through the traditions of the Palestinian Judaism of their day. His death was a crisis for this faith and the understanding of God in those traditions. His death called into question basic beliefs about God and about divine care of those who are faithful to God. It was a religious crisis that provided the opportunity for a revelation of God. The revelatory power of Jesus' death lies in the way it shattered one religious vision to make way for a new one. It must be investigated as an event in the history of religions. It marked the end of one mode of believing in God and the creation of a new one.

The Death of Jesus and the Apocalyptic Vision

Christian theology has had difficulty in seeing Jesus as a believing person who faced the threats to life and its meaning by faith in God. Christological reflection is tempted to retreat into a psychological docetism that conceives of Jesus as not needing faith because of his divine nature.[3] Yet, he lived, as do all human beings, in search of meaning and hope before the threats to life. Jesus is not only the object of faith but was himself a person of faith. His death came as a question of faith for him and for his disciples.

The Gospels do not picture Jesus as facing death in calm assurance of its outcome. Death is the crisis that threatens faith, as it does for all people. Jesus died in despair, and his followers fled in fear and confusion. They lost the faith by which their lives had been sustained and oriented. In death Jesus was abandoned by the God to whom he had been fully open. This fact raises not only the psychological question of how to have faith in face of terrifying tragedy, it raises the theological question, what does it mean to affirm the deity of God in light of the death of Jesus, in whom God was actually present?" What is the nature of a God who leaves the Just One, who lived in such perfect communion with God as to call God "my Father," to die on the cross? To deal with this question, it is necessary to look at the religious context through which Jesus and his followers expressed their faith.

Judaism in first-century Palestine was a religion deeply concerned with the vindication of the covenant promises that God had made to the people of Israel. Its fundamental faith in Yahweh as the Lord of history had been repeatedly called into question by the convulsions of its own history. Its most persistent religious problem was finding a spiritually and affectively convincing theodicy. To maintain faith in Yahweh as the God who acts in human affairs, it is necessary to know where and how the goodness and power of God are evident. The search for a convincing theodicy was not an intellectual puzzle for an elite. It was the fundamental religious problem for the community. The lack of a convincing theodicy threatened a breakdown of faith.

A fundamental theodicy had been given by the Deuteronomic writers of ancient Israel. Despite trenchant criticisms of their overly simple approach to the problem of evil in Job and the Psalms, the notion of "sin and suffer, do good and prosper" was a staple of the religious outlook in Jesus' times. Jesus had issued disclaimers of all attempts to justify God's ways by use of an overly neat calculus between a person's sins, or even those of one's parents, and suffering (John 9:3; Luke 13:1–5). Yet it is evident that religion in that day, as in the present, turned to the common-sense appeal of the Deuteronomic vision of how God governed the world.

The prophetic literature from Amos to Second Isaiah posed another option. Hebrew prophetism placed the problem of the sufferings of the people in a larger ethical context than had the Deuteronomists. The destiny of the people of God was given meaning by the universal rule of Yahweh over all nations. As the Lord of history, Yahweh works God's righteous will in judgment and redemption in a pattern more complex than that of the life of an individual or single community. It is Yahweh who moves the nations, even when they are not conscious of it, to bring about the judgment and redemption of God's people. Yahweh was no longer a local cultic deity but the universal ruler whose power did not depend upon human willingness to act. God could raise up for divine purposes even the pagan conqueror Cyrus to do God's work because divine power is not limited by human decisions (Isa. 44:28–45:1).

At the same time, the prophetic literature was able to plumb the meaning of suffering to new depth. The righteous will of Yahweh was at work through the sufferings of the people to redeem humankind (Isa. 52:13–53:12). Yet the problem of theodicy remained and deepened, as the promised return of the people to Jerusalem at the end of the Babylonian Exile was not the eschatological event that would bring in the gentiles and herald the reign of God on earth. The vicissitudes of postexilic Judaism were not the vindication of the sufferings of the people. Suffering continued as national life dwindled to the disappearing point under Persian, Greek, and Roman rule. The response to this growing obscurity of the justice and power of God was the emergence of the apocalyptic vision within Judaism.

The apocalyptic vision, with its origins in Zoroastrianism, came into Judaism during the exilic and postexilic period. The late Old Testament literature and noncanonical writings are replete with visions of a coming apocalypse.[4] The justice of God was to be vindicated and God's covenant promises to Israel fulfilled in a great cosmic catastrophe that would bring the present age to an end. From its Jewish sources, it found its way into primitive Christianity. This apocalyptic literature deals with the emergence of ultimate salvation by the direct action of God at the end of history. It approaches the promise of salvation at the end of history through a unique dualism. The apocalyptic dualism is not the hellenistic philosophical dualism between flesh and spirit. Instead it is temporal. "The present evil age" in which we now live is sharply distinguished from "the age to come" or "the messianic age" which will appear when God acts finally to destroy evil and institute a righteous reign in the kingdom of God. The apocalyptic vision enables the faithful to live in the present evil age so as to be able to enter the messianic age of salvation at the end of history.

The imagery of apocalypticism is bizarre and its scenario of the coming end times complex. The apocalyptic vision strains the imagination to the breaking point to describe the final act of salvation that rescues the people of God from the overwhelming forces threatening them. Modern rationalism has seen apocalypticism as a vision of desperation in which moral and cosmic order are cast aside. But this is to misunderstand its theology. The apocalyptic vision arms the believer to face the brokenness of present existence with the conviction that history is hastening to its turning point. The present becomes bearable because divine intervention to vindicate moral order is but a short time away.

The apocalyptic writers hold firmly to faith in the covenant promises of Yahweh. God is the Lord, and the Holy One will save the people of God. But in face of the power of the ungodly, in this present evil age, the vindication of God's ways can only be understood by recasting the scenarios that had come from the prophets or the Deuteronomic tradition. God is still Lord of history although hideously destructive forces are now loose. Daniel is told in his visions of "the four beasts" and of "the ram and the he-goat" that the great world empires which they symbolize will be brought low to make way for the kingdom of God (Dan. 7:1–8:27). Yet God's presence is obscure now. The divine ways can no longer be traced in the movements of history but are seen only in a heavenly vision.

This world is now under the rule of Satan and the emissaries of evil. The wicked do prosper and the righteous suffer. In the apocalyptic scenario, human affairs are moving toward ever greater evils. Even the holy place of the temple will be profaned and all nature caught up in chaos (Dan. 9:27; 11:31; 12:11; and Mark 13:14). In this time, even the elect are threatened with loss of faith (Mark 13:20). Then as the dizzying paradox of faith and doubt reaches unbearable heights, there is a denouement. Direct intervention by God brings history to an end; God executes righteous judgment, rewarding the faithful with eternal felicity and the wicked with damnation. The apocalyptic literature lacks the penetrating historical analysis of Isaiah or Jeremiah. History has become irrational. The psychic atmosphere has changed because hope is wearing thin. The vision of hope is in the breaking through of the transcendent. God the obscure becomes God the revealed. "The Lord whom you seek will suddenly come to his temple," but when God comes it is in judgment (Mal. 3:1–3).

The Possibility of Faith

The apocalyptic vision is affectively significant because it provides a way to relate the present existence of the faithful to the salvation promised in the future. The apocalyptic vision makes faith a possibility. The power of evil is so strong in this present age that believers are tempted to lose faith and accept the god of this world (2 Cor. 4:4)–the Satan–as the only god. Perseverance in faith is the highest virtue and the most difficult task in apocalyptic times. Yet, if the present were completely void of meaning, hope would be impossible. There had to be some disclosure, no matter how limited, of those forces that guarantee future triumph.

Such a revelation is granted to a steadfast believer, a seer, or prophet who has a dream or vision of the heavenly realms where the goodness and power of God are evident (Dan. 7–12; 2 Esdras 3:14; Enoch 83:90; Rev. 4:1). The vision gives hope because it discloses not only the power of God but also the divine plan for the faithful to be rescued. As the seer retells this vision, the faithful are able to link the chaos and suffering of the present to the salvation to come in the future.

In the apocalyptic tradition, the power and goodness of God are real now although hidden until the end times. In this respect, biblical apocalyptic differs from modern progressive or revolutionary ideologies, or the so-called "theologies of the future."[5] These modern visions see goodness emerging in the future from within history. The apocalyptic vision does not speak of "God" coming to full reality at the end of history. For apocalyptic, the goodness and power of God exist already although they are temporarily obscured. However, this hiddenness does not mean God is unreal or powerless. The vision granted to the prophet or seer reveals the benevolence and power of God that will be vindicated at the end of history. In the present, the faithful person is to live by trust in what he or she has seen.

The apocalyptic seer is a religious hero who shares his or her vision with others so as to allow them to have faith. Daniel, who resisted the blandishments and threats of the powers of this age, is granted a vision of how God will resolve the impenetrable riddle of history. Daniel's vision of the beasts, who represent the great nations, reaffirms the prophetic understanding of history. The movement of the nations is in response to God's righteous judgment although this is unknown to them. The focus of the vision, however, is upon the Son of Man to whom sovereignty in the coming kingdom is given (Dan. 7:13–18). This Son of Man is the embodiment of the martyred "saints of the Most High" to whom kingly authority is given. In other words, he is a direct link between the suffering people and the future triumph. The powerless will be empowered by God through the suffering Son of Man. God will be vindicated, and the people of God will be vindicated for their faithfulness when justice is established at the final judgment.

The vision the seer imparts to the faithful is of a realm of power and goodness that has its being in itself. This is the heavenly realm, the transcendent, where God and the saints dwell. This realm is not the outcome of history, nor is it produced by human action, but it exists already. However, it is involved, in secret ways, in the affairs of history that now seem so chaotic. The rulers of this age, despite their present strength, have a destiny of judgment and destruction guided secretly by God. Ultimately, the faithful will be saved from them. Yet the saints do not create this salvation. It exists already, now hidden, only to be revealed in the future. The vision shows how God will be faithful to God's covenant promises. The covenant God is still the Protector God who rescues the elect people as Yahweh did of old, even as the earthly signs of divine rule fade. The scenario by which the Protector God acts has shifted, but the covenant is still to be honored.

Having been told the apocalyptic vision, the religious crisis of the person living in a time of suffering and injustice is not fully resolved. The question that remains is personal. What does it mean to live in the present by trust in God as revealed in the vision? This is not a question for the unrighteous because they have already chosen the god of this present evil age—the Satan—as their god. The righteous person who remains faithful to the hidden God asks how to persevere. The answer is that the saints of the Most High must be willing to surrender everything, even life itself, in response to their faith in God and the divine promise of the future. However, the apocalyptic vision does not leave the faithful without guidance in this crucial matter.

The seer, like Daniel, Enoch, or John of Patmos, through whom the vision of the divine power and goodness comes, is a religious hero who has resisted the temptation and threats to faithfulness and has been protected by God. The one who trusts God lives by a curious alternation between passivity and assertion. The prophetic seer is actively self-assertive in obeying God, even courting conflict with the earthly rulers (Dan. 1:8–16; 3:16–18; Luke 9:51; 22:42). Nonetheless, in the moment of testing when facing death, the hero is resigned to the will of God. One's trust must be perfect, for until the very last moment, the hero does not know if God's will is life or death.

Jesus as Hero

The apocalyptic scenario of the prophet or seer who brings knowledge of the divine triumph over evil is a particular form of the myth of the religious hero. Anthropological and history of religions research has identified psychological and mythological patterns of the religious hero in many traditions. Ernest Becker (1924–74), Mircea Eliade (b. 1907), Joseph Campbell (b. 1904), and Gerhard van der Leeuw (1890–1950) have identified both underlying psychological patterns and the particular historical manifestations of the hero figure.[6] The common pattern of the hero may be simply stated. The hero separates himself or herself from the world of common life to encounter the dangerous forces, natural and supernatural, that threaten and destroy human life. The hero rejects compromise with corrupting worldly forces and goes through severe trials by the evil powers. In these trials, the hero is taken beyond the limits of this world to encounter demonic, supernatural forces in the realm of death. Despite the encounter with death, the hero is delivered because the hero is seized by the Holy. Finally, the hero returns from this adventure with his new-found knowledge of ultimate reality to bestow the blessings of salvation on people.

The myth has many variations in different cultures and religious traditions. However, the myth has a core of commonality that char-

acterizes it, in Campbell's judgment, as a "monomyth" whose underlying unity may be identified in different historical settings. While
not necessarily accepting either the psychological interpretation of
the myth given by Campbell, nor even the existentialist recension of
it given by Becker, the identification of the religious pattern of the
hero has great importance in understanding late Judaism and early
Christianity. The identification of the pattern of the hero allows a
new understanding of the historical context of revelation in Jesus.
Revelation occurs at the point at which Jesus assumed the role of the
religious hero and yet ultimately went beyond it. The analysis of
Jesus in light of the hero shows that revelation both assumes the
patterns of human religiousness and yet precipitates a crisis within
them. The death of Jesus revealed God precisely because it caused a
religious crisis. It marked the end of one way to have faith in God.

The hero discloses human existence at its interface with the transcendent. The hero displays how humankind may be transformed by
sharing in the divine power of being. Gerhard van der Leeuw sees
the hero-saint as one who "is seized by grace and his very nature
transformed."[7] The hero has so touched the realm of the divine as to
be able to bring its power of being to humankind. This makes the
hero a savior. Such a pattern lies behind some of the earliest Christologies of exaltation that talk of how Jesus is given a new and higher
status because of his willingness to go through suffering and death
(Acts 2:36; Phil. 2:9–11). In a related fashion, Eliade describes the
hero as one who bridges the time between the present and the time of
redemption.[8] The hero does what only God can do. The hero can be
present in all times.

The hero is religiously vital because he or she discloses the invulnerability of the person of faith who draws strength from the transcendent world. By claiming none of the powers of this age for
protection, the apocalyptic hero lives only through the powers of the
age to come. The transformation of the hero through horrendous
trials discloses what divine grace can do for those who live by faith.
But this invulnerability of the hero is uncovered only in extremity.
The hero goes into the trial without the assurance of victory. The
willingness to take this risk is what makes one a savior. He or she
returns to everyday life and entrusts the hard-won knowledge of the

ultimate security of the self in the transcendent to others who could not obtain it themselves.

The religious hero who is seer of the apocalyptic tradition removes himself or herself from the ordinary means of security to encounter demonic evil in both human and supernatural forms. In unbending obedience to the will of God, the hero comes under the condemnation of death from the rulers of this present evil age. When rescued dramatically by divine intervention, the hero returns with a saving message to be shared with others. Daniel forsakes comfort and security to brave the wrath of Nebuchadnezzar; he is given visions of the heavenly realm and is finally brought to the edge of death. He is rescued by God and then returns to share his saving vision with others. Shadrach, Meshach, and Abednego reject compromising their obedience to God and are carried to the brink of death from which they are preserved by the coming of one "like a son of the gods" into the fiery furnace (Dan. 3:25). They return to wrest a confession of their God from Nebuchadnezzar, who promotes them to high places.

Jesus lives as the hero in the apocalyptic scenario. He separated himself from the security of family in response to God's call and came into conflict with the power of a despotic state and hostile religious leaders. He was tempted to capitulate to the demonic powers but walked steadfastly through the terrors of a demon-infested world. He entered conflicts confident that God the Protector would be faithful to him. Through the agony of the Garden of Gethsemane, the abandonment by the disciples, the trial by torture, and the cross, the hero is tested. Jesus is the religious hero who lives by faith and is enabled to go to meet his destiny on the cross. He is obedient to the point at which human rescue is no longer possible. In this, he follows the classical pattern of the hero who withdraws from all means of security to encounter the demonic. But is the classical model of the religious hero really fulfilled in him?

In the apocalyptic vision, God the Protector is vindicated by saving the hero at the last moment through dramatic supernatural intervention. At the last moment, according to the apocalyptic scenario, Jesus the Just One will be rescued by God and thereby give reassurance that God's sovereignty, although hidden, is still real. In the case of Jesus, however, the paradigm of the religious hero was broken. The Hero whose faith allowed him to call God "my Father" died on the cross forsaken by the God in whom he trusted.

Jesus did not die in serene confidence. His death was the antithesis of the "beautiful death" of Socrates who dies in confidence of the rightness of his vision of reality. Jesus died in dereliction because the covenant promises of protection had not been honored. The one who was the embodiment of the saving remnant was not saved by the Protector God of his people. The heavenly Father was not able to save Jesus from death. As Jurgen Moltmann put it, "The fact that Jesus had been abandoned by God raises for him the question of God's deity."[9]

The deity of God in the Jewish apocalyptic tradition was the divine ability to vindicate the covenant promises for the care and protection of God's people. In the case of Jesus, God the Protector had failed. The mouths of the lions were not stopped; the heat of the furnace was not cooled; no legions of angels came to overwhelm the crucifiers; a sky-chariot did not translate him to heaven; nor was Jesus able to elude the soldiers to leave some other hapless victim in his place on the cross. Religious legends of a final escape have no place in the canonical Gospels although found in the gnostic gospels and the *Qur'an.* At the last moment there was no dramatic supernatural intervention, only the death of the One who had trusted fully in God. The resolution of the problem of evil of the apocalyptic tradition collapsed.

The faithful community that followed Jesus was shattered. The disciple Cleopas summed up their hope as he returned in despair to Emmaus, "But we had hoped that he was the one to redeem Israel" (Luke 24:21). The "prophet mighty in deed and word before God and all the people" was not rescued but died (Luke 24:19). They believed his death to be final. The sign event—the saving of Jesus— that was to provide the necessary assurance in this time of waiting for the kingdom failed. With it, the last thin thread which supported belief in God the Protector was broken. The disciples fled in panic, not simply out of fear of reprisals against them, but in despair over the loss of God. The disciples did not wait serenely for a resurrection that was assured. Their hopes were at an end.

The Sinlessness of Christ

The steadfast faithfulness of Jesus as the religious hero had been reinterpreted by Christian theology in the doctrine of the sinlessness of Christ. Central to the remembrance of Jesus were traditions that witness to his perfect obedience to the will of God. Before either threat or allurements from this-worldly rulers and the demonic forces, Jesus was steadfast in his obedience. The interpretation of the New Testament witness to the sinlessness of Jesus by later Christian theology lifted these traditions out of their historical setting. The context of Jesus' struggles was Jewish legal piety, while the context of the doctrine of the sinlessness of Christ is the later Christian doctrine of original sin, particularly in its Augustinian form. This shift made the sinlessness of Christ a doctrinal conundrum that undermines the humanity of Jesus. Augustine argued that in the fall human nature was vitiated by sin so that all humankind became "a mass of perdition" destined to pass on not simply the tendency to sin but the actual guilt of sin. Original sin is propagated not by imitation but by human generation. Hence the only release from original sin is in one who stands outside the natural lineage of the human family.[10] When it is asserted that someone sinless has appeared, the relation of such a person to the rest of humankind has to be qualified. It becomes difficult in this setting to believe Jesus ever encountered temptation. This line of thinking led ultimately to the Roman Catholic dogma of the Immaculate Conception of the Virgin Mary.

In the context of Jewish piety, faithfulness to the law of God is a possibility for human beings. There is such a thing as a just person before God. Abraham intercedes for the righteous in Sodom. Job maintains his righteousness despite the efforts to call his goodness into question. Esdras, Enoch, Daniel, and the seers of the apocalyptic writings are just men. The problem of evil with which the apocalyptic literature wrestles is set by the existence of truly just people to whom God has made promises of protection. The just person has a standing before God and is repeatedly promised rewards in this life and beatitude in the life to come. There is nothing inconsistent with the full humanity of Jesus in his fulfilling the role of the just person as defined in Jewish piety. It is Jesus' faithfulness to the will of God that precipitated the religious crisis posed for him and his disciples by the cross. The sinlessness of Jesus means that he never turned aside from the will of God.

By contrast, with Jewish piety, there can really be no problem of theodicy in light of the Augustinian doctrine of original sin that has dominated Christian theology. There are no just people, according to the Augustinian doctrine. Christian piety, unlike that of Judaism, has no legends about "the Last of the Just."[11] All people are born in sin and deserve the wrath of God. The question of whether punishment comes now, or later in hell, is immaterial. The real question is how does anyone escape total punishment? It is not the problem of evil but the possibility of salvation which is the problematic in light of the Augustinian doctrine of original sin.

Sinlessness is not a construction imposed upon Jesus to qualify his humanity. It is part of the historical context for the revelatory crisis of the cross. Jesus was sinless because he did not break the law. Like Job, Christ rejected the accusations of lawbreaking thrust upon him. He went to his encounter with God in the whirlwind of the cross, but Jesus was not given the just person's reward, so conveniently supplied in the editorial refinements of the Job epic. Jesus did not receive the reward, nor did he finally see God. He died instead in dereliction.

Beyond the Heroic

Evidences of belief in Jesus as the Hero are to be found throughout Christian theology and piety. The hero motif has been particularly important in the Reformation and in contemporary liberation theologies. Jesus' crucifixion came about historically because he was condemned as a blasphemer by the religious community and a subversive by the state. He was, on this level, a victim of the demonic perversions of religion and nationhood that infect human history. His death is the interpretive principle to illumine the persistent conflicts between gospel and law, faith and accumulated tradition that mark all religious history. This vision of Jesus was crucial for the Reformation. Jesus is the creative archetype of the heroic reformer who violates the tradition of his religious community in the name of the Higher Reality to which the tradition points (Matt. 5:20).[12] Jesus challenged the particular religious law of his time to proclaim the law of God. He contested the way the Sabbath was observed or ritual purity preserved to point to the higher righteousness required by God. His willing acceptance of death is the affirmation of faith against the accumulated traditions of the religious community perverted by self-interest. His conflict with the religious leaders who guarded the tradition of his community is the assertion of the freedom of the person of faith against every demonic form taken by the holy.

The crucifixion of Jesus is the discernment point for understanding the meaning of political revolution.[13] The cross is the witness to the transfiguration of politics that comes when human freedom is asserted against political power. Jesus is the resistance hero who claimed the power of the powerless by choosing death over perversion of his humanity. He is the fully human voice speaking against the demonic claims of the absolute state to set the conditions of human life. To leave the Christological question in this form, however, is to stand with the disciples as they sought for Jesus' identity in the heroic: "Some say John the Baptist, others say Elijah, and others Jeremiah or one of the prophets" (Matt. 16:14).

Christology deals with the impact of Jesus on human affairs, but finally it must deal with the question of God and Christ's deity. Christologically viewed, the crucifixion of Jesus meant the death of the Protector God of the old covenant and the collapse of the apocalyptic scenario. In Christian theology to speak of "a crucified God" is not merely a homiletical hyperbole. It is the way to identify the point of revelation. The death of Jesus was the religious crisis in which God, the Source of salvation, had failed the One who had trusted God fully. The old covenant had been closed, and the new one had not yet been opened.

The resurrection of Jesus from the dead is an unconditional new beginning. As the unexpectedly new beginning, it did not fill the disciples with comfort and peace, but, as Mark tells us, with terror and awe in the face of the breaking in of a Beyond that they had thought to be empty. The resurrection was the verification of Jesus' words about a new covenant that was being formed. Resurrection is not the master illustration of immortality nor proof that human life extends beyond physical death. Resurrection is the emergence of a new ground for human hope.

Resurrection could not have occurred without crucifixion. Crucifixion, in this light, is what Paul Tillich (1886–1965) called the "critical" preparation for revelation. Yet it is more than that. The crucifixion is itself revelation.[14] It is the revelation of the death of the tribal, Protector God. It is the death of all schemes to protect the self, even those based on God. While this death was transformed in resurrection, Christian faith insists that this death is an abiding part of resurrection. The faithful person cannot go around the cross to resurrection. This is why people are baptized into the death of Jesus as well as into his resurrection. This is why Paul spoke of the church being under the cross. Myths of invulnerability have no place in Christian faith.

Death, the collapse of meaning, is integral to the finding of a new and higher meaning. The salvation offered through the cross of Christ does not build on already existing centers of security; it destroys them. This is why in the Christian faith the means for finding salvation is repentance, the death to self, the forsaking of already existing centers of security to make one open to new being. The death of Jesus gives final revelatory meaning to his own words: "If anyone wishes to be a follower of mine, he must leave self behind; day after day he must take up his cross, and come with me. Whoever cares for his own safety is lost; but if a man will let himself be lost for my sake, that man is safe" (Luke 9:23–24, NEB). The death of Jesus means that the root metaphor for the meaning of God is not "protection" but "transformation."

5

Jesus and the History of God

The History of God

God is confessed by Christians to be eternal and immutable. Thomas Aquinas (c. 1225–74) gave classic theological expression to this confession:

> Hence, as God is supremely immutable, it supremely belongs to Him to be eternal. Nor is He eternal only, but He is His own eternity; whereas no other being is its own duration, since it is not its own being. Now God is His own uniform being; and hence, as He is His own essence, so He is His own eternity.[1]

Not only has Christian theology spoken of the eternal immutability of God, so has Christian piety because the assurance of faith is grounded in the divine changelessness. Henry F. Lyte (1793–1847) taught generations of Christians to sing of the assurance that comes from the unchanging God standing in contrast to the ever-changing world.

> Swift to its close ebbs out life's little day;
> Earth's joys grow dim; its glories pass away;
> Change and decay in all around I see,
> O Thou, who changest not, abide with me.[2]

This is only one dimension of the Christian faith in God.

Christians hold another conviction about God to be every bit as vital as that of faith in God's eternal unchangeableness. The revelation of God is given through mighty acts in history. The history of the Hebrew people, the life, death, and resurrection of Jesus are the revelation of God. God acting to save people has constituted these events as a *Heilsgeschichte,* a history of salvation, that discloses who God is and how God acts. It is not through mystic contemplation or intellectual reflection that God is self-revealed in the biblical understanding but through a particular series of events.

However, this history of salvation is real history marked by change and variation. The history of salvation is not the disclosure of archetypal myths for ever-recurring events but a series of unique events revealing God's will and way in the world. This history of revelation is marked by change in which the understanding of God and human response to God have taken different patterns at different times. This history is not simply a chronicle of the events of ancient Hebrew life or that of Jesus and his earliest followers. It is a history that includes human response to these events as the self-disclosure of God. Christians see a pattern of prophetic promise and fulfillment in the history of revelation that reaches its resolution in Jesus Christ. The Christian community affirms the finality of the revelation in Jesus and subsumes all earlier disclosures of God under the supreme revelation given in him. "In many and various ways God spoke of old to our fathers by the prophets; but in these last days he has spoken to us by a Son" (Heb. 1:1–2a).

Human responses to divine revelation carry the indelible stamp of the different cultures in which people have offered their worship and obedience to the holy. God was known in very different ways in tenth-century-B.C. Canaan from those in first-century-A.D. Palestine or sixteenth-century Europe or twentieth-century America. As historians have made the religions of the past known, the possibility of finding some consistent core of ideas about God has become problematic, if not impossible. However, modern theology has maintained belief in an eternal, immutable God despite all these changes. It has done this by a natural theology whose roots are in mysticism and philosophical monism.[3] Changes in the vision of God, it is argued, are but differing attempts of the human mind to grope after the divine. God is eternal and unchangeable; it is only the human words used to describe the divine that change. There is in this viewpoint, strictly speaking, no history of God but only a history of the human attempts to know God. Christians in the modern period have used this kind of natural theology to explain the profusion of religions found in the world, as well as the bewildering variety of beliefs within the church. There can be a history of the human consciousness of God but not of God's selfhood. Is such a position tenable?

The critique of this kind of theology by Karl Barth and the dialectical theologians focused Christian theology afresh on revelation in history as its source.[4] However, this return to the concrete history of revelation as the center of theology posed the problem of historical change in its most acute form. The logic of the dilemma is evident.

(1) Christian faith finds knowledge of God in God's revelation and not in the human search for God.

(2) Divine revelation takes place in and through history. There is, to use the patristic term, "a historical economy" to revelation. The history of the Hebrew people and of Jesus of Nazareth are the means of divine self-disclosure.

(3) Therefore, changes within this history are part of God's revelation. Revelation historically unfolded from its beginnings in ancient Israel to its fulfillment in the life, death, and resurrection of Jesus Christ. Revelation moved from promise to fulfillment. The revelation of God utilized different means of disclosure. God spoke through the prophetic word and Wisdom literature. Ultimately, God is known by the incarnation. The content of this revelation was changing also. This historical unfolding of revelation must be taken seriously by theology. The changes in understanding of God are not merely changes in human words. *For if God is who God is in revelation, then the unfolding history of revelation is also the history of God.* History is not irrelevant to God, nor does it merely define actions external to the divine life. There is a history to the divine being, so that any definition of God as eternal and unchangeable cannot deny the flux of the concrete history by which God is known.

For Christian faith, the history of revelation was given its decisive turn in Jesus. The specific question is, what did the death of Jesus reveal about God? If Jesus is confessed, in Nicene terms, as "being of one substance with the Father," then the question of his death is no longer only the question of a human death. It is a question about God. How is the eternal God involved in the death of "his only begotten Son"? To deal with this question, one must place it in the larger context of the divine self-disclosure as found in the Old Testament.

The Disclosure of the Divine Name

The Old Testament records the history of God as made known among the Hebrew people. Historical research shows that "Yahweh," whom Israel worshiped as the One God, Lord, and Creator of the heavens and earth, reached full definition through an interplay of the faith of Israel with the polytheistic world of ancient Near Eastern religions. Historically, Israel derived worship of Yahweh from the Kenites or Midianites, in critical interaction with the worship of the Canaanite El. Yahweh emerged through a complex history to a final status in the faith of Israel as the one and only God by historical acts of deliverance of the people of God in which there was revelation.[5] Yahweh revealed the divine name, that is, God's being and nature, by overcoming all previous names by which God had been called. This process of revelation by overcoming the earlier divine names is reflected in biblical phrases that refer to Yahweh as "King of kings," "Lord of lords," and "God of gods." The whole pantheon of divine "kings," "lords," or "gods" by which God had been known were overcome in the mighty acts of Yahweh through which Yahweh emerged as the one Lord and King. The emergence of Yahweh as the Lord in the radical monotheism of the Hebrews was a process in which the God of the people transcended God's self to disclose the divine name.[6]

The history of Yahwism is not that of a tribal God arbitrarily elevated to universalism. Yahweh's universalism is God's existence as the God who is able to call into question every characterization of God (Isa. 42:8). In the biblical vision, God is the "Lord of lords" before whom no divine name is so sacred that it cannot be called into question (Deut. 10:17; Ps. 136:2,3; Enoch 9:4; and 1 Tim. 6:15). Yahweh is the "King of kings" before whom no covenant is so sacrosanct as to be exempt from divine judgment. Every relationship to God is subject to righteous judgment, as well as sustaining power. Theologically viewed, the divine name itself—*YHWH*, "I will be what I will be" or "I cause to be what I cause to be"—is not the name of a particular clan's God among the gods so much as the naming of the divine life that claims and transforms every name, be they the mythopoetic names of the ancient Near Eastern religions or the philosophical, abstract names of systematic theology.

From the earliest traditions in which Yahweh was still related to the other gods until the radical monotheism of the prophets where the Lord is the one and only God, Yahweh emerged with ever-greater clarity through divine actions for God's people. God is not the unnameable Beyond. God is the One who has transformed every name in acts of salvation. Yahweh was first God among the gods, then the victorious God over the gods, and finally the only God. The names or powers of the gods are not relativized and rejected as in mysticism but transformed and appropriated. In the struggle against the fertility gods of Canaan, the prophets do not place Yahweh beyond concern for fertile fields, expanding herds, and large families. Instead, as Hosea proclaims, Yahweh has preempted the role of the Baalim in granting fertility to the faithful people and their land (Hos. 2:16–23). Yahweh has not withdrawn from the world, nor is God disinterested in the act of creating. Yahweh is the true Creator rather than the gods to whom people have wrongly attributed creation.

For Christian faith, Jesus stands in this series of mighty acts of revelation as their consummation. He is the final revelation of God who brings the process by which the divine name is disclosed to completion in his life, death, and resurrection. This completion of revelation, however, was more than a mere summing up. It involved also the most profound transformation in the knowledge of God. Jesus revealed God in a radically new way by his crucifixion. His death negated the magical God, the *deus ex machina* of popular religiousness, who could come with the "legions of angels" to save the faithful Son. In death, Jesus revealed the "God of gods." He revealed God as the One who embraces death in the powerlessness of love and by this embrace, triumphs over death.

Via Negativa or Plan of God

The way in which Yahweh transcends the name "God of gods" is fundamentally different from negative theologies of the philosophical and mystical traditions. The *via negativa* in Advaitic

Hinduism, hellenistic philosophical religion, and Christian mystical theology relativizes every name of God as the way of pointing to the true God who is beyond all names. Every name or attribute of God is finally transcended in the *via negativa* because God is the Beyond (Ger., *Urgrund* or *Ungrund*) which is greater than any human name that can be given. The divine reality is known by philosophy and mystic thought in a process of abstraction that finally rids the name of God of all particularity. The search for God is along the ladder of analogy in which each human name to describe God—Father, Lord, Protector, King—is first affirmed but finally denied as inadequate. For the mystic, God is Father. Yet the fatherhood of God is ultimately different from that of any human father we know. All human fathers are weak and dependent creatures whose love and care of their children is flawed by self-interest. No matter what word is used to name God, the mystic reiterates, as did the sages of the *Upanishads,* that it is "not that, not that" (Sans., *"neti, neti"*). The divine ground is beyond all "form and name" *(rupa kai nama)* as the motionless sea of pure being that defies all naming. The divine is the ground that exists in itself without attributes (*nirguna*) and is only intimated by imperfect signs to those who remain in the world of empirical reality.[7] The Neoplatonist mystic Plotinus could only speak of his unitive vision of God as being "alone with the Alone."

Yahwism has a very different vision at its heart. Yahweh is not the passive ground but the actor in the drama of history. The naming of God is not the result of the human search but of God's own acts of self-disclosure. It is not the believer who calls the divine names into question; it is very God. The mighty acts of judgment and redemption reveal God's name (Exod. 15:11; Deut. 32:31; Ps. 82; 1 Sam. 2:2–10) until Jesus appears as the one with "the name which is above every name" (Phil. 2:9). The transcending of the divine names is not along the route of negation, the *via negativa,* but is the plan of God's own self-disclosure. In the New Testament, the death and resurrection of Jesus are the final revelation of the divine name. In his death all previous names of God die, and in his resurrection they are transcended in the name that is given to Jesus. This name is above every name (Phil. 2:9; Acts 2:36; Rev. 19:12–13). In this view, the death of Jesus is not a contingency in which the evil forces of this world seek to erase his name from human remembrance. Instead, the death of Jesus is part of the plan of God whereby Yahweh makes the saving name known to the nations by overcoming the limitations of all previous names. The key to this paradoxical assertion is in the New Testament claim that the death of Jesus was "by the deliberate will and plan of God" (Acts 2:23, NEB).

"By the deliberate will and plan of God"

The New Testament weaves together the dual themes of divine plan and human responsibility in its accounts of the crucifixion. Jesus was given up to death "by the deliberate will and plan of God." As the Passion announcements of the Gospels make clear, "the Son of man must *[dei]* suffer many things . . . and be killed" (Mark 8:31–33; 9:31–32; 10:32–33 with parallels in Matt. and Luke). The necessity of Christ's death was not historical determinism, nor did it arise from human cunning. It is God's plan. To resist this, Jesus told Peter, is to be "not on the side of God, but of men" (Mark 8:33). Yet the New Testament also says that Jesus was killed "by lawless men" who are responsible for his death (Acts 2:23). He died through the collusion of historical forces in a tragedy not only moral—the death of a good man by the forces of injustice—but also religious. Jesus died seeking to fulfill the will of God, and with him perished the apocalyptic vision that had allowed men and women to hope amid tragedy. His death meant the death of the tribal Protector God through whom humans had sought safety.

However, the notion of divine necessity at work in the death of Jesus flies in the face of common sense. How could God be thought to do this? Mark and Luke, reflecting editorially on the Passion announcements, said that when the disciples heard "that the Son of man must suffer many things . . . and be killed," they "did not understand the saying, and they were afraid to ask him" (Mark 9:31–32). Acceptance of the death of Jesus as part of God's plan was possible only in Christ's resurrection from the dead. Without the resurrection, the question of Jesus' death could only be raised as an ethical question—the death of a just man—not a theological one. Yet the divine necessity in Christ's death was at work before the resurrection. It was not a post facto interpretation placed on his death.

Hence, the contradiction must be faced that God conspired to become the crucified God. To conceptualize this requires a way of thinking about God that goes beyond either naive personalism that sees God as a kind of larger-than-life human being, or philosophical monism that blots out the human face of God in pale abstractions. There is a dynamism in God. God is the living God who changes and reacts to what goes on. This dynamism cannot be made into an impersonal divine force, nor can it be perverted into the arbitrary will of a despot. The God of love is the one known through the death of Jesus. The approach to understanding the divine necessity in the death of Jesus can be made by looking at the history of God's covenanting activity because the death of Jesus marked the transition from the old covenant to the new covenant.

Covenants Old and New

Covenant is one of the most basic categories by which ancient Israel and the early church interpreted their response to the revelation of God. The concept of covenant has been used to structure Christian theology ever since. Theologically the Christian community has been concerned with the transition from the old covenant, made through Abraham and Moses, to the new covenant made in Jesus Christ. However, there is an older pre-Abrahamic covenant with Noah that God made with the whole of humankind. It is a universal covenant. The special covenant of revelation made with Abraham has its setting and meaning within the larger universal covenant made through Noah. In the covenant with Noah, God entered into a relationship of care with all humanity (Gen. 9:8–17).[8] The rainbow, which is the sign of the covenant with Noah, is the sign of peace. Yahweh had put aside "the bow of war" never to bring it against the whole human family again. The covenant with Noah promises God's faithfulness to all people in the regularity of the seasons, preservation from annihilation, and the gift of mastery over the created order (Gen. 8:20–9:17). Within this universal covenant, Yahweh made a special covenant of revelation with the Hebrew people to witness to God and the divine will in the world. The covenant of disclosure did not abrogate the covenant with Noah. Rather, the covenant with Israel takes on its importance within the universal covenant of Noah.

The covenant with the Hebrew people had two dimensions. It was a covenant of protection in which God promises to preserve the people God elected. It was also a covenant of revelation in which the people disclose the being and will of God to the nations. The protection was set in the context of the covenant call to reveal God for the blessing of the nations. "I will bless those who bless you, and him who curses you I will curse; and by you all the families of the earth shall bless themselves" (Gen. 12:3). It was under this covenant of protection and revelation that Jesus lived and carried out his ministry. By his faithfulness, he made known the name of God and so lived by trust in God's faithfulness to him. The covenant promises had been reinterpreted many times in the history of Israel. However, they remained intact although the means of their fulfillment were now understood in dramatically supernatural ways by the apocalyptic writers.

The death of Jesus was a crisis for this covenant theology. Jesus had been faithful. He had made the name of God known through his words and deeds. But this faithfulness was not met by an answering faithfulness from God in deliverance from the cross. Having been willing to face death with no human means of protection, Jesus was not rescued but died in dereliction. The death of Jesus struck a blow at the covenant of protection. It was a theological problem of the starkest proportions. If Yahweh had not been faithful to the covenant, then God was not who Yahweh said God was in revelation.

What was at issue in the death of Jesus was the threatened failure of God to keep covenant promises. The breakdown of the covenant of protection, as understood in the apocalyptic vision, marked the end of one modality of faith. It posed a religious crisis for Yahwism in which its fundamental conception of God's relationship to humankind had collapsed. The death of Jesus was the death of God for those who knew God through the covenant of protection. But the breakdown of that covenant was also the occasion for a new revelation of God to emerge. It is this emergence which is announced in Jesus' promise of a new covenant.

Jesus' promise of a "new covenant in my blood" is the consummation of the covenanting activity that had started with Noah and centered in revelation with the election of Israel. Among the ancient Israelites, there was a growing awareness of the ambiguities of their existence as a special covenant people. As was made clear in the prophetic preaching, the people could expect no protection because they had failed to fulfill the will of God. The covenant with the Hebrew people was one linked concretely to the life of the nation with all its ambiguities and failures. God's covenant functioned through fallible kings and sinful priests. It was dependent on a temple cultus in the eyes of many, while others thought it was linked indissolubly to their destiny as a nation-state. By the sixth century, Jeremiah looked for a new covenant in which the limitations and the external forms of the present covenant would be transcended by inwardness and the immediate presence of God given through "a new covenant" (Jer. 31:31). As the writer of the Epistle to the Hebrews was to comment on this passage centuries later, "In speaking of a new covenant he [Jeremiah] treats the first as obsolete" (Heb. 8:13). The old covenant through its dependence on external legal and ceremonial means of grace pointed beyond itself to a new covenant in which the universality of God would be given full expression. The time will come when the people will be given "a new heart" and "a new spirit" so they may seek the commandments of God (Ezek. 11:19–21).

The old covenant had become morally ambiguous as the people of Israel turned to God for protection while rejecting their mission of living by God's law. The covenant was persistently misused as a means by which a particular people hoped to gain blessings from God. Originally the covenant had been formed so that the people could witness to God, and through their witness "all the nations of the earth shall bless themselves." However, instead of becoming "a light to lighten the Gentiles" (Luke 2:32, KJV; cf. Isa. 42:6; 49:6), the people became preoccupied with their own particularity and their prerogatives before God. The moral ambiguity of one people being the particular people of God was heightened. In apocalypticism, this

moral ambiguity reached its peak. The saints were pictured as waiting eagerly for retribution to be meted out to their opponents. Vengeance against enemies was to be coupled with blessings to only one
particular people in the apocalyptic vision of divine judgment. If
salvation were to come to others, it had to come through the Hebrew
people to whose capital humankind would be drawn, happy to
accept the role of servants. Tragically, the church later took over this
same misappropriation of the covenant to justify its oppression of
the Jews and its militancy against other religions. Jesus' opposition
to this kind of vengeful particularism is clear. The protection given
by God is of a very different order. "Whoever cares for his own
safety is lost; but if a man will let himself be lost for my sake, that
man is safe" (Luke 9:25, NEB).

It was necessary to pass beyond the old covenant. But a change
in covenant means theological change because God is who God is in
covenant relationships. To speak of a new covenant means that God
has revealed new aspects of the divine being and will. This revelation
of God through the new covenant is in the death of Jesus. To say that
the death of Jesus was "by the deliberate plan and will of God" is to
say that in it God acted self-transcendently. God, "the Lord of
lords," the "God of gods," reveals divine absoluteness by transcending all conceptions of God in revelation. The deity of God is
not in changelessness. In the death of Jesus, God the Protector was
negated. This negation was willed by God and so opened the way to
disclose God as the One who makes new. The resurrection of Jesus
from the dead defined this new meaning of God as transformation.
Christ is the one who gives new being to humankind even in the grip
of death.

By his death, Jesus opened the new covenant. The Christian
eucharist is the covenant rite in which the community of faith proclaims the death of Jesus until he comes (1 Cor. 11:26). The eucharistic meal sets forth the dual orientation of the new covenant. The new
covenant is oriented to the saving events of the past, and it is oriented forward to the coming of the kingdom. The new covenant is
grounded in the death of Jesus. His blood poured out in death is "the
new covenant." The body that was broken "is for you." But the new
covenant points to the future. The Eucharist is to be celebrated

during this interim until Christ comes and the full power of the kingdom is made known. In the present, the fullness of this new covenant remains hidden, except for those who live by faith and have "foretastes" of the kingdom, of which sharing in the eucharist is one. What has been made known is the power that will bring in the kingdom. It is the power of God to transform everything, even death.

The Assurance of Salvation

Difficult religious and theological problems surround all talk about God's involvement in suffering and death. What does it mean to say God is open to change and is vulnerable to the world? Where is the certainty of salvation with a God who is vulnerable to death? What is the constancy of a God who is self-transcendent? Such questions have rightfully been asked of the theologians, ancient or modern, who speak of God coming under suffering and death. The early church condemned as heretical the Patripassianist teachers, such as Sabellius and Praxeas because in making God the Father vulnerable to the sufferings and death of the Son, they had undercut the saving power of God. The logic behind the rejection by the church of these early forms of Patripassianist theology is clear. If God is subject to suffering and death, then God is open to being overcome by these destructive powers. This remains the key objection to the contemporary process theologies.

Despite the critical shortcomings in their Christology, the Patripassianists were able to maintain the unity of God against all efforts to make Jesus a subordinate deity on his own. They understood that the divinity of Christ would not be real if his power of being were different from that of God. It is impossible to preserve the integrity of Jesus' divine nature by weakening the bond between God the Father and the incarnate Son. The Patripassianists held to the reality of Jesus' suffering and death against all Gnostic attempts to make the Passion a mere appearance that in no way touched his personal center. But the model they proposed for conceptualizing God was too simple. They understood the unity of God as simple, undifferentiated arithmetical oneness. Their vision of God was one of God as a vast undifferentiated sea of pure being. Their model was inherently static. The complex interplay of personal life never rippled the sea of divine being. What was needed was a more complex model for interpreting the dynamic quality of God in relation to the world. Later trinitarianism developed such a model by its insistence upon the differentiation of Father from Son and Holy Spirit, while maintaining the unity of God through the dynamic coinherence of the persons of the Trinity with one another. The Patripassianists had no way to conceptualize the complexity of change in God because for them Father and Son were identical. There was no dynamic in the divine life that could overcome the tragic consequences of God's sharing human life. Yet the Patripassianist theology saw clearly the importance of God's real sharing in the sufferings of Jesus. This was an aspect of Christian faith that had to be retained and given more adequate conceptualization.

Cyril of Alexandria (d. 444) started to move the conceptualization of God's involvement in suffering and death into a fresh perspective. He spoke a word of contemporary importance beyond the fifth-century fight against Nestorius and the Christologies that wanted to separate the human from the divine in Jesus. Cyril rejected the Nestorian Christology that divided the impassible Word of God and the suffering person Jesus save for a similarity of will between the two. There could be no split between Jesus and the Word of God, he argued, else there would have been no incarnation and, hence, no salvation. Instead, there is a coinherence between God and human being in the Christ. But to affirm this it became necessary to state more exactly how God is involved in the suffering and death of Jesus. Cyril approached the problem by reflecting on the way in which God participated in suffering:

> We confess that the Son himself who was born of God the Father, God only-begotten, suffered in the flesh for our sake according to the scriptures, even though by his own nature he is impassible, and he appropriated impassibly in his crucified body the sufferings of his own flesh. By the grace of God he tasted death for all, having given over his own body to death, even though by nature he is life and resurrection.[9]

The notion of God "suffering [*pathe*] . . . impassibly [*'apathos*]" is a paradoxical formulation that points to the character of God's involvement in suffering and death. For human beings, suffering is more than physical discomfort or anxiety. Suffering poses the threat of extinction. Suffering distorts and may finally destroy the personal center. Psychic and physical pain can decimate the self, leading to annihilation in suicide or affective numbness. While there is a good deal of popular religious rhetoric about how suffering ennobles character, the opposite is more often the case. Suffering calls into question self-identity because it erodes the personal center and the moral values that so fragilely support it. By contrast, in God there is a ground of healing that goes beyond the most destructive demonic forces in the world, even death itself. Hence, God may be involved in suffering, but God is not distorted or annihilated by this suffering. God the Lord suffers impassibly. Divine participation in suffering is real, but God is not finally a victim of the destructive power of suffering. The divine self-identity remains intact. The deity of God is not vitiated in suffering and death because as Lord the power of transformation is greater than the power of suffering or death. There is no need to preserve the deity of God by making God aloof from the world. The deity of God is revealed in the divine freedom to become involved in suffering and yet not to be distorted by it. God is and remains the Savior God.

The conceptualization of God's involvement in suffering and death requires a complex logic. God cannot be thought of as a simple undifferentiated unity. This is where the Patripassianists failed. Neither can the power of God be made into sheer willfulness before which moral distinctions are lost. God is not a despot who arbitrarily imposes suffering. There is, instead, a mutuality in God's relationship with the world. There is a richness and complexity to the divine life. All that the biblical witness says about God requires a conceptual framework that can comprehend this dynamic life. This emerged in the doctrine of the Trinity. Classical trinitarianism provides a means for relating the involvement of God in suffering and death to the constancy of the divine will of love.

The Faithfulness of God

In confessing its faith in God as Trinity, the church is affirming belief in the living God. In this regard, Christian trinitarianism is the heir to prophetic Yahwism. God is living, dynamic process, not the sea of undifferentiated being, so divine eternality and immutability are not stases but the constancy of the divine will of love. To use the language of Hebrew prophetism, God is faithful to covenant promises. Yahweh is the saving God by virtue of this faithfulness. However, after the death of Jesus the ways in which God shows faithfulness were given fresh expression in the new covenant. God's faithfulness is not shown in the avoidance of death but by the unique character of divine involvement with death. Such a notion could not be fitted into the theistic logic inherited from hellenism that tied the eternal character of God to changelessness. What was needed was a way of conceptualizing the divine constancy of purpose in relation to a dynamic, responsive life.

In trinitarianism, God is not "the Father" who chooses at some time to be self-revealed through the Son and the Spirit. Rather, God is Father, Son, and Holy Spirit together. No person of the Trinity has priority over the others; they are coeternal. Strictly speaking, in trinitarian theology, the word "God" can only be used univocally when speaking of Father, Son, and Holy Spirit together because the unity of God is that of a mutually begetting triad in which the Father begets the Son through the Spirit. Each member of the Trinity has its unique character, yet each draws its being from its relationship to the others.

God relates to the world because God is already self-related. God is involved in the alienation and reconciliation characteristic of human life because God is already a process of giving and receiving life within the Godhead. Hence, God is in revelation what God is internally. The self-imparting activity of God in revelation is not extraneous to the divine being. Hence, to say that revelation in Jesus Christ transcends previous revelation is possible because it is God who is transcending God.[10] No external power forces change on God. Change is of the essence of the divine life. In the freedom of divine love, God expresses the divine essence as love in new and fuller ways. The dialectic by which the divine name receives new definition in Jesus is the pattern of the divine life itself. There can be a real history of God because God is in essence what God is in revelation. For trinitarianism, God is living process, and so the historical unfolding of revelation is intrinsic to God. It is not the shifting attempts of humans to name God. The history of revelation is the unfolding of the divine life.

The history of God is a story that reveals the constancy of divine love. The eternal and immutable character of God is the divine will of love for the redemption of humankind. The dynamic process in God is in the fulfillment of this will of love. In a wonderful turn of phrase, Karl Barth spoke of the "holy mutability" of God.[11] By contrast, there is, he added, "an immutability about human beings" in their sin. There is a dreary sameness about the human rejection of love in the self-centeredness of sin, while there is infinite variety in God's address to humankind. There is a "holy mutability" about Christ who not only ate with sinners but finally took their sin upon himself and suffered their penalty of death (2 Cor. 5:21). God reveals divine holiness by going beyond the rules of holiness. Through the Holy Spirit, God not only speaks to each one of us personally but enters most intimately the lives of finite and sinful people to sanctify them. In all this, the church confesses that God does not become unlike God's self. To confess God as Trinity is to say that no matter how we encounter the Holy, all is of God—Father, Son, and Holy Spirit.

Power and Love

Christians use the words "power" and "love" to express their faith in the triune God. However, when these terms are used to confess the Trinity, they cannot be defined by starting with our common-sense ideas of power and love and then applying them to God. Instead, since God is in essence what God is in revelation, the divine excellences are defined not by abstraction but by the revelatory events in Jesus Christ. There is a coinherence of language between God and the revelatory history of Jesus. The attributes, or excellences, of God need to be defined in relation to one another, not in isolation. "Power" and "love" cannot be defined as opposites because, when applied to God, each serves to shape the definition of the other. The weakness of theologies that emphasize divine sovereignty is that they center the divine life in power and make love only an incidental feature of that power. The power of God revealed in Jesus is God's freedom to love. Or, to put it the other way, God is the one who loves in freedom.[12]

God loves in freedom because God's relationship to the world is one entered into freely, in grace, rather than out of necessity. God does not need the world to complete God's own incompleteness. God's relationship to the world is not symbiotic but free because God as triune is already self-related. The divine life is one of interrelated love in itself. What is expressed in the divine relatedness to the world and human history is God's gracious calling of humankind to be a covenant partner. By contrast, human love tends to be symbiotic because it proceeds out of the incompleteness and self-interestedness of human beings. Hence, there is always a certain intolerance of differences between the lover and the beloved. Agape never completely overcomes eros in human relationships. All of our love relationships lack full freedom. Christian faith affirms that God loves in freedom because divine love is graciously bestowed out of divine bounty. Since it is a love given in freedom, it has the power to create freedom in the one who is loved. The power of love is not the negation of freedom but creation of greater freedom.

The notion of power implies interaction, but power means more than that. Power also implies the capacity to fulfill a goal or purpose through this interaction. The context for defining the power of God is in the divine interaction with the world and human history. It is here that the inner-relatedness of the triune God is manifest. In this interaction, the power of God may be characterized both negatively and positively.

Negatively, the power of God is not the freedom to do anything imaginable. While God is free because the divine life is grounded in itself, this freedom is not the power of pure, unbridled possibility. It is not the freedom to be capricious. God cannot contradict the divine will of love any more than God can decide to be unjust. As Anselm (c. 1033–1109) said in his analysis of divine omnipotence, a being who is capable of lying or making what is true false would not have power but impotence, for to be capable of perversity would be to give perversity power over one.[13]

Positively, the power of God is in the divine freedom to realize the will of love in the redemption of humankind. This power is articulated in relation to the world in such a way that it does not destroy human freedom. Rather, the divine power creates freedom where it had not existed before because of the presence of sin and death. By the gift of the Spirit, God creates the freedom for sinful human beings to obey the divine will of love. By the act of divine sin-bearing on the cross, God has created freedom from sin. By the resurrection of Jesus from the dead, God has granted to humankind the possibility of freedom from death. In this way, the will of God is fulfilled. To say that God is powerful in this does not mean that God destroys human freedom, even though this freedom has been misused. God saves by creating freedom.

The cross of Christ is the disclosure of God's vulnerability to the abuses of human freedom. More than that, the cross reveals that the power of God is not to be found in the prevention of tragedy but in the transformation of the tragic consequences brought about by the misuse of human freedom. The freedom of God is supremely the power to overcome death, the worst consequence of human sin, by giving new life. Yet salvation does not mean invulnerability.

For Christian faith, the power of God to love gives the assurance of salvation. This assurance is not in the vision of God as the One unruffled by suffering and death into which the immortal soul may merge, nor is this assurance found in the picture of God as the capricious Ruler to whose will no check may be given. Rather assurance comes from historical events—the life, death, and resurrection of Jesus—as apprehended in the power of the Spirit. These events disclose the meaning of the power of God as the freedom to embrace death and finally to win over it by love. The assurance of salvation does not come from the discovery of something immortal and indestructible—a soul or divine spark—in human beings. Death is real and irreversible. Human analogies break down at this point because for us the embrace of death is final. It is dissolution into bits and pieces, absolutely beyond recall. The power of God embraces death and brings from its nonbeing new being. "God chose . . . things that are not, to bring to nothing things that are" (1 Cor. 1:28). The powers of this world, who in their might seem able to destroy all

goodness, are brought to final nothingness by the power let loose in
the death and resurrection of Jesus.

Sexism and the History of God

Feminist theologians have brought into contemporary
thought and church life the problem of how to conceive of God in
the face of the persistently male orientation of traditional language
about God. The religious symbols and ideas found in Judaism, the
classical world, and early and medieval Christendom are predom-
inantly masculine ones. As ancient Israel and the church received
God's self-disclosure, it expressed its faith and shaped its cultus by
religious symbols that were masculine. This religious language developed by the church witnesses to its unique and central faith in the
Trinity that speaks of a Father and a Son, related to one another by
the Holy Spirit. Yet if revelation has the power to call any religious
form or name into question, is it not possible to transcend the limitations of an exclusively masculine language? The question is a difficult one about which little agreement has emerged. It is always much
easier to admit theoretically that there is a distinction between revelation of God and the religious language in which we seek to witness
to that revelation than to make such a distinction in practice. Religious symbols are not invented nor prescribed by theologians. They
have a life of their own. Perhaps Naomi Goldenberg is right in
arguing that God will be conceived in feminist terms as women find
their places as central figures in the basic acts of worship of the
church.[14] Evidences of these changes are already starting to appear
in churches that have ordained women for ministerial leadership in
sacraments and preaching and not only in the helping ministries to
which women usually have been assigned. It is impossible to predict
the outcomes of these developments at this time. Yet certain things
are evident from the theological analysis of the ways in which the
revelation of God has transformed religious language in the past.

In the history of the emergence of Yahweh as the God of gods,
sexuality has been a critical question. While there are fragments of
very primitive myths about the sons of God cohabiting with human
women (Gen. 6:4), the notion of Yahweh as a literally male figure

bringing the heavenly hosts or legendary figures into existence by sexual relations was transcended at a very early stage. The key encounter was during the settlement of the land when the Israelites took up farming in Canaan. The fertility gods of the land posed a challenge to Yahweh, who was known as the God of the wilderness. As the Israelites learned farming, they learned of the need to placate the fertility gods by acts of sacrifice and worship that included cult prostitutes, both male and female. The prophetic critique of these competing cults rejected a literally masculine identity for Yahweh. Yahweh was not pictured in the prophetic literature as a consort to the female deities of fertility. While there may well have been popular hybrid Yahweh-Baal cults that pictured Yahweh as a masculine figure who impregnates a goddess of the fields, this is sharply rejected by both prophetic teachers and popular reformers, as for example in 2 Kings 23. This rejection, however, does not mean that Yahweh becomes thereby antisexual or impersonal.

The rejection of the picture of Yahweh as a masculine cult deity does not mean that Yahweh is unconcerned with fertility of field and herds nor that the gift of children is a matter left to a lower earthly plane of existence. Sexuality and fertility are powers that have been given to humankind by Yahweh, not by the Baalim from whom the people falsely seek them. Yahweh is not an impersonal power of being, devoid of sexuality. Both female and male powers are present in God. The transcending of the panoply of male and female deities by Yahweh did not negate sexuality as a power relevant to the divine. It brought these powers into the divine life from which they flow to human beings and the natural order as a means of blessing and of life. What are the implications of this development?

Theologically viewed, God may be characterized by both feminine and masculine images. In its witness to God's revelation, the Bible may speak as God: "As a father pities his children, so the LORD pities those who fear him" (Ps. 103:13), and "As one whom his mother comforts, so I will comfort you (Isa. 66:13). The critical point in the biblical use of these images is that our preexisting notion of mother and father, of female and male do not become a kind of natural theology that dictates the nature of God. Rather our language about God serves to express what God reveals of the divine being. This revelation may be expressed in a variety of images and metaphors, both female and male. God is not an undifferentiated whole whom we identify with female or male images. Rather God is the actor in history whose disclosures may be expressed in personal metaphors of both genders.

6

The Resurrection of Jesus
as the Disclosure of the Human

The Signs of the Resurrection

For the Christian community of faith, the resurrection of Jesus from the dead is the vindication of his trust in God. Jesus lived, to the end, by faith. As the power and goodness of God became increasingly obscure, Jesus was "obedient unto death, even death on a cross." Because of his acceptance of the will of God, even when it meant death, in his resurrection he was "highly exalted" and given the "name which ˙s above every name" (Phil. 2:8–9).[1] The resurrection of Jesus discloses that death is not beyond the power of God to transform. From nonbeing God brings life. Now as the Christian community of faith waits for the kingdom amidst the uncertainty of history, it lives by the realization that "death is swallowed up in victory" (1 Cor. 15:54). In the resurrection, God is revealed as the one who can redeem the vulnerability of love from the destructiveness of death. The resurrection-exaltation of Jesus is not only the vindication of God, but it is the disclosure of the human. In the risen Christ, human being has been brought into a new configuration that carries it beyond the power of sin and death. The resurrection is not the victory of a dematerialized nonhuman reality over death, nor is it the disclosure of the immortality of the soul. It is resurrection of a body. It is the transformation of human nature for which there are historical correlates. It is a historical event.

In the New Testament, the resurrection of Jesus is not an undifferentiated, vague symbol. It has a specific meaning and structure that is defined in the events that surround it. The meaning of the resurrection is found in the signs of the resurrection that provide its historical evidences. Two kinds of evidence for the historicity of the resurrection are found in the New Testament.

First, there is the evidence that comes from the experience of new life in Christ, as people respond to Christian proclamation. This new life came from personal trust in Jesus perceived as being personally present and at work in the congregation of the faithful. As Kierkegaard put it, there is no such thing as a "disciple at second-hand."[2] Because Jesus was raised from the dead, he could be known directly and not merely through historical remembrance or doctrinal affirmation. As the Risen One, Christ is present in the worship, preaching, healing, and helping ministries of the church in a direct personal fashion.

Second, there is the evidence that comes from the reports of the empty tomb and the appearances of Jesus immediately after his resurrection.

For the individual responding to the proclamation of Jesus, the experience of new being in Christ has priority. The experience of new life makes the question of the resurrection of Jesus a "live option" for faith and thought. If Jesus were not affectively and spiritually significant in human experience, reflection on the events surrounding his death would provoke little concern. For early Christians, reflection on the resurrection was not thinking about a peculiar happening, a kind of curio. It was thought about as an event fraught with power.

This priority of immediate experience as the basis of reflection has made it the custom for modern theologians to deal with the resurrection solely in terms of the new being granted the person of faith. The evidence of the empty tomb and the appearances has been shuffled aside as either misleading or irrelevant. Much modern theology sees them as later additions of a superstitious piety. Concentration on the immediate experiential aspects of the resurrection has cut theology free from making the history of the resurrection decisive for theological affirmations. In modern experiential theology, discourse on resurrection is in reality talk about the immediate experience of the community of faith. Past events may be illustrations of the experience being discussed, but they are not determinative. Lessing's "ugly broad ditch" between history and God is left unchallenged.

The historicity of the resurrection implies more than a present experience. Full investigation of the resurrection pushes necessarily to the historical events that most immediately surround it. Instead of being irrelevant additions, the empty tomb and the appearances are integral to the resurrection. They are signs that disclose the form and content of the new being in Jesus, the Risen One. The immediate, surrounding events show the resurrection to be the disclosure of the human future granted in Jesus.

On the Third Day

On the third day after Jesus' death, two facts became evident:[3] (1) the tomb in which he had been buried was found to be empty; (2) he had appeared to some of his followers. Historical access to these events is through the postresurrection narratives of the Gospels (Matt. 28; Mark 16; Luke 24; and John 20–21), Paul's report in 1 Corinthians 15, and references to Jesus' appearances found in Acts and the Epistles (for example, Acts 9:1–22; 22:3–21; 26:1–23; Gal. 1:12, 16; 2 Cor. 4:6). Obviously, reports of the empty tomb and the appearances have undergone a complex editorial development in which legendary materials were added to underline their theological significance. No final separation of a framework of uninterpreted events is possible. These events and their meaning for the life of faith closely coinhere. As Christians witnessed to their faith, they developed a narrative form that binds the historicity of the resurrection intimately to its impact on the life of faith. However, no matter how severe the problems this poses for historical analysis, the resurrection is not thereby rendered nonhistorical or mythological.

The theologically less developed report of the empty tomb in Mark 16:1–8 has an undeniable claim to authenticity. This is not the report of a wish-fulfillment. It is the report of people caught in a surprising, awesome event. The terrified disciples showed no evidence of having their most fervent expectations fulfilled. "And they went out and fled from the tomb; for trembling and astonishment had come upon them; and they said nothing to any one, for they were afraid" (Mark 16:8). The empty tomb was a radical intrusion into what the disciples had expected to find. They were struck by terror as they were unable to find the body of Jesus. Their expectations were shaped by a common human presupposition: dead people stay dead. The empty tomb broke the usual pattern of human expectations, and so it called for explanation. The empty tomb was the occasion for theological reflection, but the empty tomb was not itself an idea produced by theological reflection nor by pious expectation.

The disciples had seen their expectations of the final deliverance of humankind heralded by Jesus die with him. With him had died the apocalyptic expectation of a dramatic intervention of God to rescue the Elect One. An empty tomb had no place in their scenario for the future. In the disciples' vision of salvation, Jesus was not supposed to have died, but that scenario had ended at the cross. With the empty tomb a very different scenario was set in motion. The empty tomb was not the projection of a theological conviction onto the plane of history. It was a historical event setting in motion a new theology. The empty tomb and the appearances were the intrusion of a strange, wholly-other power into life. This intrusion was not immediately perceived as revelation by the disciples. But the historicity of this intrusion made responses to it necessary.

The empty tomb was part of the revelatory context of Jesus' resurrection. Its immediately elicited response was not faith but astonishment. In his phenomenology of religion, Gerhard van der Leeuw describes such a moment as the point at which experience is pushed beyond its limits to an encounter with revelation. This encounter occurs when a superior power is seen to be intruding into human experience. The encounter with the "Impressive Other" pushes human experience into a new realm in which the available religious metaphors and symbols have no interpretive power. In such a situation van der Leeuw writes, "Man's attitude to it is first of all *astonishment*, and ultimately *faith*."[4]

This transition from astonishment to faith must be examined in any historical analysis of the resurrection. This transition is the basis of the discontinuity between the emerging Christian piety and theology in which the resurrection became a symbol of peace, hope, and joy and the terrified astonishment of its earliest witnesses. In its later reflection, as the church started to find more fully the meaning of the

resurrection, the starkness and terror of the empty tomb were miti-
gated. Joy, peace, and hope become dominant themes in the witness
to the resurrection. The resurrection narratives of the Gospels themselves give us insight into this transition from astonishment to faith.
It is a transition in which dread before the unexpected and terror in
the face of the unknown are mingled with the joyous expectation of
the gracious breaking in of the divine.

Matthew adds a report of the appearance of Jesus to his account
of the empty tomb (Matt. 28:1–10). His narrative reflects the transition from astonishment to faith in the account of the women who
had gone to the sepulchre. Matthew reports that "they departed
quickly from the tomb with fear and great joy" (28:8). Matthew's
report takes us a step beyond the Markan tradition that focuses on
the fear associated with the empty tomb. Matthew shows how the
fear of the unexpected is now linked with the joyous expectation that
God has done a new thing. Out of deference to the historical priority
and authority of the reports of terror, Matthew does not replace
these reports of fear as did much later Christian piety. In speaking of
these witnesses to the empty tomb being filled "with fear and great
joy," Matthew is exploring a complex set of emotions that are at the
basis of the resurrection faith of the church. The empty tomb is, on
the one hand, a radical break with the past. They have lost the body
of Jesus and those visible historical links they sought to his ministry.
On the other hand, it opens before them as an expression of a new
beginning that God was making.

Luke retains the elements of fear and perplexity in his report of
the empty tomb. Yet he places the resurrection and with it the empty
tomb in the context of a prophecy by Jesus that it was to occur (Luke
24:6–9). There are reports in Luke and John of continuing skepticism about the empty tomb until the appearances clarified its
meaning (Luke 24:22–27; John 20:24–29). In a reversal of male
chauvinism in religious matters, Luke gives priority to the women in
their encounter with the empty tomb and belief in the resurrection.
The Apostles remain skeptical or blind to the report of Mary Magdalene, Joanna, Mary the mother of James, and the other women
(Luke 24:11, 16–24). Unlike Luke, John links the visit to the tomb
with belief in the resurrection for at least some of the disciples.

However, John leaves the empty tomb as the occasion for sorrow and confusion on the part of Mary Magdalene until Jesus appears to her (John 20:11–18). By contrast with the Synoptics, John specifically dissociates the resurrection from previous prophecies of it. According to John, "as yet they did not know the scripture, that he must rise from the dead" (20:9). Seeing the crucifixion and resurrection as the fulfillment of Scripture was only possible in light of their actual occurrence. Instead of being part of a previously conceived plan, the empty tomb is an intrusion that occasioned perplexity. Despite the late date of the Fourth Gospel and its tendency to subsume the events of Jesus' life into its theology of incarnation, the historical claim of the empty tomb as the breakthrough of the unexpected persists.

The empty tomb posed questions not only for Jesus' disciples but also for his opponents. The empty tomb was part of the context in which the resurrection was proclaimed by early Christians. But the emptiness of the tomb was still a matter to be dealt with by those who claimed the death of Jesus had ended his ministry in defeat. The traces of a Jewish polemic against the Christian preaching of Jesus' resurrection are found in the story of the guards placed at the tomb (Matt. 27:62–66; 28:11–15) and stories of his body having been stolen or surreptitiously disposed of. The argument was over just how the tomb became empty. The important point is that both those who affirmed that God raised Jesus from the dead and those who claimed that someone stole his body had a common starting point in the empty tomb itself. Yet the empty tomb is not the resurrection; it is a necessary correlate of the resurrection.

"And He Appeared . . ."

While the empty tomb is a basic historical correlate of the resurrection, the appearances of Jesus were needed to clarify the nature of resurrection. The appearances establish continuity between Jesus the Crucified and the Risen One. Without this identity there would have been no vindication of Jesus' faith in God. Yet, even in their earliest and simplest form, the appearance accounts are open to a variety of explanations that undercut their historicity and importance as revelation. Were not the appearances legendary expressions of a longing, wishful memory of the beloved teacher?

Two persistent difficulties beset such interpretations and point in a very different direction.

First, there is no evidence of those psychological conditions in the disciples that would produce wish-fulfilling visions of Jesus. He had been discredited by his death. He was the One "who was to save Israel," but with his death his mission had failed. The disciples had fled in fear and despair, leaving only a small group to take responsibility for his proper burial. The appearances were intrusions breaking in from an unexpected direction. At times, people were so unprepared for the appearances that they were unable to recognize Jesus until by some familiar gesture or word he made himself known (Luke 24:16, 30–31; John 20:14, 16).

Second, Jesus was proclaimed in terms of the resurrection from the dead in Jerusalem within a short time after his death. The appearances and the empty tomb were basic to Christian preaching of the resurrection from the dead. Such preaching would have been impossible if the tomb still contained the body or if the body could be produced by opponents to refute the basic claim of the Christian preaching.[5]

There remains in the New Testament a lack of clarity as to the exact extent of the appearances. The emerging theology of the church limited them to the period between Easter and Pentecost, after which the modality of the divine disclosure shifted. Primacy was no longer given to the risen Christ but to the Holy Spirit. However, Paul extended the appearances to include the one granted to him long after Pentecost. The risen Christ established him as an Apostle to the gentiles. For Paul, the risen Christ and the Holy Spirit were viewed, functionally at least, as interchangeable in their power to bring people to share in new being (2 Cor. 3:17). No exact limit may be set to the appearances. They were grouped close to the beginning of the church to clarify the revelation of new life in Christ.

The appearance stories, like those of the empty tomb, went through a development as they were integrated into the theology of the new community of faith. The later recensions of the appearance reports dropped the element of surprise and sudden intrusion.

Instead the appearances are related to the life of the congregation with its preaching and sacraments. The Emmaus appearance, for example, was related to the preaching and eucharistic worship in which Jesus is recognized by the church. "He was known to them in the breaking of the bread," and his presence was affirmed as the Scriptures were interpreted (Luke 24:27, 35). The crucial question is not whether there was theological development and legendary interpretation. The question is whether these theological developments gave rise to the appearance accounts, or whether the appearances set in motion this theological development. There were neither psychological bounds nor historical parallels to suggest that the appearances were created by the resurrection theology. In their earliest form, the appearance reports are marked by the element of surprise, even of intrusion, from beyond the expectations of the disciples. The appearances were later recognized as the beginning of the new aeon, the age of the kingdom, precisely because they were a radically new beginning, beyond the realm of the expected.

The Form of New Being

Both the power and the form of the new being given in Jesus' resurrection are indicated by the empty tomb and the appearances. The appearances show Jesus' resurrection as the emergence of a form of new being in which bodily existence is not discarded but rather enters into newness. To reject the historicity of the empty tomb and the appearances is to transform the resurrection into the source of a very different kind of salvation, namely, a salvation irrelevant to historical life. Without its historical correlates, resurrection becomes the emergence of a new understanding of human existence disconnected from the historical conditions that create our consciousness. To be sure, sharing in Christ does bring a change of consciousness, but this change is related to the bodily, historical conditions that are the substratum of consciousness. The difficulty in modern interpretations of the resurrection, be they liberal Protestant or existentialist, is their separation of resurrection from its basis in the biophysical, historical dimensions of human existence. The resurrection of Jesus is not merely a symbol for the emergence of a new set of values, a new form of consciousness, or a new source of meaning disconnected from changes in nature and history. The resurrection is the transformation of all aspects of life by God. The resurrection is the disclosure of a world open to God on all levels of its existence both physical and spiritual.

Resurrection in a World Open to God

The basis of the interpretations of the resurrection since the eighteenth century has been the scientific world view that had its foundation in Isaac Newton (1642–1727) and the classical physics he developed. The world was pictured by this science as a rigidly determined mechanism in which each and every event could be explained by a comprehensive set of laws. Newton and many early modern scientists believed that these laws were created by God and that God could from time to time interfere with them for some good and noble purpose. Eventually, however, both scientists and philosophers came to believe that God would not interfere with these laws. They were perfect and needed no change or modification to reveal God's ways. The physical world moved in all its complexity by inexorable laws. What could change were the values, ideals, and consciousness of people as they lived in this mechanistically determined world. In this scheme the universe is closed on the physical level while human consciousness remains open to God. Hence, the intellectually sensitive theologians of modernity concluded that the resurrection of Jesus was not an event in the world of empirical reality but an event in human consciousness. The resurrection symbolized the emergence of a new "God-consciousness," to use Schleiermacher's phrase, into which human beings may enter. Yet because the world is a fully determined physical mechanism, this new human consciousness is not dependent on something that happened in empirical reality. Human consciousness asserts meaning in isolation from the natural processes that sustain it.[6]

Contemporary scientific thought raises two questions about this line of reasoning that has been so influential in modern theology.

(1) The scheme of explanation in contemporary science does not picture the universe as a closed system determined by a set of mech-

anistic laws. The so-called "laws of physics" are statistical general-
izations that predict the behavior of a limited group of happenings.
There are patterns of expectations for understanding how events are
related to one another. Apples still fall off trees with an acceleration
equal to the force of gravity. When the world is studied in other
ways, however, either in the realm of the subatomic particle or on the
level of the passage of light through space-time, very different patterns of expectation are found. There is openness in the world as it
moves toward the future.

(2) The new research into brain physiology has shown that it is
impossible to conceive human thought as isolated from the biologi-
cal-chemical structures of the human nervous system. Mind is more
than the delicately balanced equations of the chemistry of the brain,
but mind is grounded in and shaped by its biochemical structures.

While it is true that consciousness is not fully determined by the
substratum of social, political, economic, and biological processes in
which human beings share, human consciousness does not exist in
isolation from its roots in the biological and historical conditions
that create human life. A change in the underlying conditions of
consciousness is the ground for a change in consciousness. The resurrection of Jesus is the creation of a new ground for consciousness.
It is a reconfiguration of human reality by a uniquely close relationship to God. Resurrection is the disclosure that the world is open to
the transforming power of God on all levels of being. The absoluteness of resurrection as the ground of redemption is its all-inclusive
nature.

The early church interpreted the resurrection through the understanding of the creation and consummation of the world mediated to
it from first-century Judaism. In this interpretive framework, human
spiritual and intellectual activities are unified with the biological,
social, and historical dimensions of existence. This Jewish-apocalyptic world view is the antithesis of the hellenistic philosophical dualism that divides body from soul. It also contradicts the nineteenth-
century scientific notion of a bifurcated universe in which spiritual
and mental activity are separated from their basis in the physical
world.

Creation is complex with many levels or dimensions of reality.

Faith in God as Creator is belief that God is the source of all dimensions of reality, and because of this, they are good. Yet creation is now under the power of sin and death which have perverted but not destroyed its goodness. Hence, creation is oriented toward the future in which it will enter the freedom of God in consummation (Rom. 8:19–21). The early church quickly rejected any docetic view of Jesus because God as Creator is the source of all existence, physical as well as nonphysical. Belief in God as Creator is also the rejection of the modern notion of the world as a closed system. God was not simply present at the beginning of the process, whenever that may have been. Events in the world are now accessible to God. In this view of creation, final salvation as disclosed in the resurrection of Jesus is the transformation of the created order, not escape from it.

From the perspective of a theology of creation and consummation, the resurrection is the event that brings the world to consummation, but the resurrection is to be distinguished from those religious schemes of salvation based on escape from the created order or its negation. Resurrection is not salvation by liberation from the world of history and material process. It is also to be distinguished from all views of salvation as enlightenment that frees a person from attachment to this world by the realization of its voidness. It is not the gift of a salvation over against the world and its powers. Resurrection is re-creation. It is a salvation in, through, and for the world. However, the resurrection of Jesus is not the continuance of creation as it now exists. Resurrection is not the resuscitation of a corpse nor the continuation of the present level of human life. It is the emerging of a new level of existence. In this sense, the resurrection of Jesus is neither "physical" nor "spiritual," as these terms have been traditionally defined.

Modern religious conservatives have tried to defend the reality of the resurrection by insisting on a so-called "physical" resurrection, while liberal religion has espoused various versions of a "spiritual" resurrection. The arguments between proponents of a "physical" versus a "spiritual" resurrection have actually obscured what took place. It was not a "physical" resurrection because the body of Jesus was not resuscitated to more of the same kind of life. If there is an account in the New Testament of a "physical" resurrection, it is the resurrection of Lazarus. His corpse was resuscitated to a continued life on the same level of being as before his death. He still lived under the power of sin and death. Eventually, he had to die a second time. The history of religions brings us many such reports of temporary reversals of physical death, but these are not what is described in the New Testament witness to Christ's resurrection. Jesus did not come from the grave to face death again at some later time, nor were his appearances merely a repetition of his previous life.

One finds both continuity and discontinuity in the resurrection appearance stories. They show the resurrected Jesus as no longer living under the limitations of space and time as he did before. Yet the term "spiritual" resurrection is also an inadequate characterization because in popular speech "spiritual" carries the connotation of a realm separated from the physical. The common-sense definition of "spiritual" has come to mean that which is less real than the physical. It refers to the realm of ideas, feelings, or imagination. Hence, a "spiritual" resurrection implies the continuation of Jesus' vivid personal influence or deeply impressed teachings on his disciples. Such interpretations exclude that which is bodily as irrelevant or outside the power of salvation. By contrast, the appearance stories of the Gospels point to a new level of human life beyond the split between the "physical" and the "spiritual."

Viewing the resurrection as transformation of human nature brings the postresurrection appearance narratives into new perspective. These narratives are marked by a perplexing alternation between the concrete, material aspects of some appearances (Luke 24:39, 42–43; John 20:27) and the immateriality of others—passing through closed doors, movement over long distances (Luke 24:31–36; Mark 16:7; John 20:19).[7] The interpretation of these passages does not fit within the usual definitions of either "physical" or "spiritual." The tendency in modern exegesis has been to reject as later additions the accounts that stress the concrete nature of the appearance, while interpreting the others in terms of the continuing psychological impact of Jesus. Yet such a separation is misleading. When viewed as a whole, the appearance narratives point to the emergence of new possibilities for human existence. They describe a transformation in which human nature is no longer bound by the limits that characterize life presently. They witness to an existence within space and time yet beyond the limitations of space and time as presently known. In other words, the resurrection of Jesus is neither the resuscitation of a corpse nor the appearance of an apparition. Jesus moved with a new freedom, no longer bound by space and time, yet he is still within space and time.

The Resurrection of the Body

The term used by the New Testament to talk about Jesus' resurrection is "bodily." This term needs to be characterized carefully.[8] To say the resurrection of Jesus was "a resurrection of the body" means there was continuity between his existence as a man of first-century Palestine and the One encountered as risen Lord. Along with this continuity, there was also change. This is possible because the "body" is not, in New Testament terms, just the biological framework within which human life is lived. "Body" is the locus of human being. It is the total configuration of the human and is not open to being split into flesh and spirit. However, the body can exist in various relationships and, hence, can be expressed in different ways.

The "bodily" resurrection of Jesus is characterized by a transition from a "physical body" to a "spiritual body" (1 Cor. 15:42–50). The transition is not based on a philosophical dualism that separates the material from the spiritual but on the eschatological transition from the present age to the age of the kingdom. The present age is "physical." In it, men and women live "by the flesh," that is, in dependence on their own powers and abilities. In the age of the kingdom, people will live "by the Spirit," that is, no longer out of their own powers but by the Holy Spirit who is the power of the new age.

"Spiritual" means "by the power of the Holy Spirit," the power of the age to come. The word "spiritual" is not an adjective to characterize nonmaterial, "spooklike" being. The realm of the Spirit is still bodily. It is the realm of fulfilled persons, not the realm in which the personal is obliterated. In biblical terms, the nonmaterial is the "chaos" or "void" that preceded creation, not "the fulness of being" (*pleroma*) that emerges in the consummation when God shall be "all in all" (1 Cor. 15:28, JB). The "spiritual," or "life lived in the power of the Holy Spirit," is the fulfillment of matter. The resurrection of Jesus was the transformation of bodily existence from life within its present limitations to life within the kingdom of God.

If the body of Jesus had been excluded from the resurrection, salvation in him would be very different. It would be a partial salvation that could ignore human needs for food, health, clean environment, and social order because, it could then be argued, these are "material" concerns. Such a salvation would be concerned with the rescue of some immortal fragment in men and women. However, the material did not fall on the "junk heap" in resurrection but was released from bondage to sin and death to enter a new freedom.[9] In Jesus, the transformation which the faithful await in the future is already complete. In his miracles and in the postresurrection appearances, he disclosed the powers that a transformed humanity will have.

Jesus and Human Fulfillment

In Jesus the potential given to humankind in creation was realized. It was realized through the uniquely intimate relationship between the human and divine that characterize his being. This is what is meant in the classical Christologies as the hypostatic union of the two natures of Christ. The outcome of the hypostatic union of the human and divine natures of Christ is the release of the human potential. In Jesus there was a sharing of attributes (*communicatio idiomatum*) between the two natures that gave rise to his personal being. This coinherence made possible the emergence of the full potentiality of the human, not its absorption into the divine. In Jesus a human life is rendered fully human by the intimacy of the relationship to God. But the human is not lost in God. In the words of the Definition of Chalcedon, the two natures exist "without confusing the two natures, without transmuting one nature into the other." In this view, the miracles and the resurrection of Jesus are not docetic rejections of his humanity but the disclosure of what it means to be fully human. The resurrection from the dead speaks of the release of human powers by the action of God. But the human remains human. What is gone are the limitations that have hindered humans from being fully human. The power for this release was given by the resurrection of Jesus; its full actualization will come in the kingdom of God.

The irony of the human potential, as we now encounter it, is that it lies beyond our power to release it. Caught in bondage to sin and death, the potential of humankind for love, community, and meaning is glimpsed in moments of vision, but this vision is mocked by everyday life. As we imagine what we could be, we are forced to admit that the visionary's utopia or the release from tension and despair promised by psychological techniques remain outside of human powers. In this respect, the rejection of modern social and psychological utopianism by the realism of neo-orthodox theology is well taken. However, there is a potentiality given to humankind in creation that is not destroyed by sin and may be realized. "It does not yet appear what we shall be," but no exertion of human powers as they now exist can reach this potential. The fulfillment of humankind is "not because of works, lest any man should boast" (Eph. 2:9). It cannot be accomplished "by the flesh" or "in the world," but it is a gift of grace that God has given "by the Spirit" and is found "in Christ." The human fulfillment offered in Jesus needs careful delineation. Human beings are not fulfilling themselves by the inspiration of Jesus as an example. Rather, humankind is being fulfilled through sharing in the transformed humanity of Jesus as risen Lord.

With this perspective, it is possible to reexamine the biblical witness to Jesus in a new light. It is not necessary to strip away layers of tradition to find a historical picture of Jesus that fits the empirical definition of human nature as it now exists. Rather, it becomes possible to interpret the New Testament witness to Jesus as the disclosure of the human future. Many accounts in the Gospels suggest themselves for such interpretations. The miracle stories do not deny his full humanity; instead, they disclose human powers presently unknown to us (John 14:12). The resurrection is the key event in the revelation of human nature. It shapes everything else. The resurrection of Jesus is not only the source but also the pattern of human renewal (Rom. 6:5; Phil. 3:21). In Paul's terms, "just as we have borne the image of the man of dust, we shall also bear the image of the man of heaven" (1 Cor. 15:49). Through resurrection, women and men may move from their present existence in the power of sin and death to a transcendent life, lived now in the power of the divine.

In resurrection, Jesus came into a new relationship with space and time. The postresurrection appearances give clues to the meaning of this relationship. Jesus still existed within space and time, but he was not bound by them. At the present level of human development, we have concrete personal being by virtue of existing within space and time. We have a locus set by the perimeter of our bodies. As human beings, we are not ubiquitous. At any given moment, we are in one particular place and not another. We live in this time and not in the past or in the future. It is this characteristic that gives our lives their peculiar quality and meaning. Finitude sets the boundaries of human life. The pain of estrangement and the joy of reunion, the threat of death, and the hope for victory over death spring from our finitude. Life is limited by time, and human relationships are limited by distance. The bittersweet quality of human life is witness to the limitations under which it is lived.

To live within the limits of space and time is the basis of personal existence as we know it. Yet, at the same time, human self-transcendence points beyond this kind of life. Men and women envisage new forms of being free of these limitations. Human life is lived out of the awareness that "it does not yet appear what we shall be." Great difficulty attends the characterization of this new being. What really would such an existence be?

Mystical religion and pantheistic philosophies have characterized the new being as the rejection of existence in space and time. The Neoplatonic mystic Plotinus spoke of the ultimate state of unity with the divine as escape from the human to be "alone with the Alone." In Advaitic Hinduism, ultimate redemption is liberation (Sans., *mukti, moksha*) in which the empirical self is transcended and the true self (*Atman*) realizes its unity with the divine ground of being (*Brahman*). The Buddhist conception of ultimate salvation as nirvana pushes the logic of redemption by loss of the self to its ultimate point. Nirvana is the state of unattachment in which the self is transcended by the realization of voidness (*sunyata*). So total is this self-transcendence that Theravada Buddhism is able to speak of redemption as the realization of the not-self (*anatta*). Human beings are saved by being freed of finite existence in favor of an infinite, eternal being. The root metaphors of salvation in these traditions are those concerned with the loss of the self in voidness or the absorption of the self into the divine ground. Salvation is likened to a tiny drop of water falling into the ocean or the flame of a candle being lost in the light of the sun.[10]

A different set of basic metaphors for salvation is found in the witness to the resurrection in the New Testament. The metaphors of salvation are those of transformation, not absorption or fusion of subject and object. Even in redemption, the human and divine exist without confusion, without change. In redemption there is coinherence between the divine and human but not identity. Time and space are not absorbed into the divine infinity. Instead, the new being that emerges in the resurrection of Jesus displays a twofold relationship to space and time. Existence is *in* space and time but not *under* the power of space and time. There is still personal existence. The post-resurrection appearances of Jesus point to a new level of human life. Space and time do not prevent the personal presence of the Risen One. The closed door is no block to the coming of Jesus, yet the One who is present gives concrete evidence to Thomas that he is Jesus the crucified (John 20:19–28). Jesus is revealed as risen to the disciples at Emmaus and, at the same time, to those in Jerusalem (Luke 24:31–34). Yet this passage rejects the idea that this was an apparition. The continuity of the Risen One with the crucified Jesus and the concrete bodily character of the appearance is asserted (Luke 24:37–43; John 20:24–29). Even while appearing in Jerusalem, the risen Jesus promises to meet with disciples in Galilee (Matt. 28:10).

Estrangement across time and space have been overcome in resurrection. This is why the resurrection of Jesus is called the victory over death. It is the breaking down of time as the barrier that separates the living from the dead. Now we know the dead as having existed only in the past, while we exist in the present. In the kingdom, all live in the future given by God. Resurrection is the victory over estrangement caused by space in which the boundary between that which is mine and that which is yours is overcome. The animosity created by the space between what is yours and what is mine is no longer a barrier to community. It is the victory over the limits that set people off from one another. This victory, accomplished in the resurrection of Jesus, will be actualized for all people in the kingdom of God through the resurrection of the dead. Yet even now the resurrection life overcomes separation and creates unity where there had been none (Eph. 2:14–16). The victory over time and space forms the basis for a new kind of human community. Life in the kingdom will make universal those intimate forms of community that are now prefigured in marriage and the family (Luke 20:35).

The fulfilled humanity of the kingdom stands in continuity with present human existence. It is "bodily" existence and, hence, includes life in community. The vision of ultimate salvation is social—the kingdom of God, the city of God. The new humanity of the kingdom represents a "quantum leap" in human development to a level of life on which our present existence is transformed. However, preconditions of such a leap exist already 'n numan life by virtue of our own creation by God. Yet such a leap will be a break with life as it now exists.

The emergence of a fulfilled humanity will, in New Testament terms, come in judgment and redemption. It will be an emergence through tragedy. What now exists is dominated by the power of sin and death so that it must die in order for the new to emerge in resurrection. There is here no easy escalator of progressivism that promises release from the ambiguity of life. Rather there is the promise of a victory through the tragic. In this regard, the biblical images of judgment are crucial. Judgment is the refiner's fire, the threshing of grain at the time of harvest (Rev. 3:18; Matt. 3:12). There are suffering and loss but finally not destruction because the refined gold and the pure grain are the outcome. The consuming fires and the beating flails are the means of a release for further growth and greater use. They are not irrational destruction. Human redemption does not come by avoiding tragedy, nor does it come in spite of tragedy. It comes through tragedy. The movement is one from death to resurrection.

The Christian vision of new life in Christ, in the kingdom of God, breaks fresh ground in the impasse between the secular and religious ideologies of the future. Unlike secular visions of hope, the fulfillment of human evolution does not come by a simple progressivism in which, step by step, the powers of human betterment fulfill themselves. Neither is human fulfillment in the release of nonmaterial "souls" from a world that is going to destruction, as in some religious visions. Fulfillment will come from beyond, from God, from powers beyond human ability or control, but it will not be unnatural, unworldly, or inhuman. It will be the fulfillment of the human. To use the Pauline metaphor, in salvation we shall not "be unclothed, but clothed upon" (2 Cor. 5:4, KJV).[11]

Living in the present, the goal of human fulfillment remains uncertain. The lines of human development may point to fulfillment, or they may point to contradiction and the destruction of human life. The present is what the apocalyptic tradition calls the time of "the woes," with its "wars and rumors of wars," its false prophets and unnatural events. In such a time, to believe in a more human future is an act of faith. The assertion of faith now allows the faithful person to realize that these woes are not the death throes of the golden age. They are "the birth-pangs" of the kingdom (Mark 13:8). Such a faith is possible because in Jesus Christ the shape and the power of that future have been revealed. This future exists already in him. To have faith in Christ is to start to share in that future now.

PART II

A Transition Point

The Broadening Question

The small but highly visible countermissionary movement of the non-Christian religions to Europe and the Americas has created an awareness of options for a faith other than our own. The choice is no longer between secular indifference and a commitment to Christian faith. A host of competing religions have emerged as possibilities. These new religious options make the spiritual quest in contemporary life more complex than ever before. Alongside the airport sadhus and storefront meditation centers has been the tremendous growth in the academic study of other religions. The Scriptures, philosophies, art, and institutions of Hinduism, Buddhism, Islam, as well as the traditional religions of Africa, China, Japan, and South America are becoming known in ever greater depth. Scholarly work has started to unfold the spiritual, intellectual, and artistic resources of these traditions as an integral part of the human story. College and university religion departments are no longer organized just around biblical studies and the ethical values of the Judeo-Christian tradition but now offer many options for studying all the religious traditions of humankind.

There is today the growing awareness that the study of these religions is not affectively detached or spiritually indifferent. People are finding resonances in a variety of religious traditions that speak to their deepest searchings. Many confess that nonwestern traditions have spoken more deeply to them than have the churches and synagogues from which they come. Religious pluralism has become an intellectual and spiritual fact for contemporary life. This pluralism raises the most difficult questions for those who seek to maintain belief in the universality of the Lordship of Jesus Christ. How is it possible to maintain the universality of Christianity when it is only one religion among many? For the Christian, in a way not true for devotees of many other religions, the questions posed by religious pluralism are never merely detached queries. They are questions that probe the center of faith.

Personal awareness is inevitably a part of grappling with the meaning of other religions for Christian faith. For me, this awareness came at the end of a seminar held at the Punjabi University in Patiala, India, as part of the quincentenary celebration of the birth of Guru Nanak, founder of the Sikh tradition. This seminar had brought together scholars from many religious communities all over the world to share their perspectives on Guru Nanak, the great spiritual teacher of sixteenth-century India.[1] Guru Nanak had struggled to reconcile the warring religious factions of Hindus and Muslims by an ethical monotheism. On the one hand, the tone of the seminar had been shaped by the irenic spirit of Nanak in whose name it had been convoked. On the other hand, there was dissonance, so well known in such gatherings, as different perspectives and faith commitments shaped opinions that came into frequent conflict.

The Punjabi University had arranged, at the conclusion of the seminar, for the participants to visit the great shrine sites of the Sikhs. The pilgrimages ended late one afternoon at the Golden Temple in Amritsar, the principal shrine of Sikhism, at which pilgrims gather daily to worship and bathe in the huge pool that surrounds it. As dusk crept over the Temple environs, the evening service of *Rahiras* was finished by the reciting of the *Ardas* or supplication, a prayer to be said morning and evening and at the beginning and conclusion of family, public, or personal religious devotions. The prayer is punctuated by responses from the people, which were signaled at the Golden Temple by the striking of a huge drum. Thousands of worshipers surrounded the pool, while the Temple, now filled to overflowing, was still reflecting the last glints of sunlight. As the great drum sound reverberated over the water, the people repeated in a hushed roar, "*Wahiguru, Wahiguru.*"

The response means "Wonderful [Punjabi, *Wah*] Spiritual Teacher [*Guru*]." Their response was a remembrance of Nanak, their first guru, and his successors in the chain of ten gurus whose words are in the *Guru Granth Sahib*, the Scripture of the Sikhs. The response invoked the presence of these teachers and the transcendent power of their words for this community of faith, but it is more than that. *Wahiguru* not only invokes the great teachers of that tradition, it is also a name for God unique to the Sikh tradition. It affirms that beyond all human teachers, God alone is the "Wonderful Teacher." To confess God as *Wahiguru* is to acknowledge that all human words about God are but echoes of that eternal word (Punjabi, *Shabud*) spoken by God Almighty. God alone can make God known by the inner testimony of the divine Spirit. Knowledge of God is not the reward for human wisdom or piety but a gracious gift of God in self-revelation. God is the "Wonderful Teacher" who dwells not only in heaven, or in the great and noble spiritual teachers, but is present in everyone telling us of the divine. All human words about God are but resonances of the divine Word.

Standing there at the edge of the pool in this great company of worshipers, I felt the awe of the presence of the Holy. These words spoken by pilgrims, pious or worldly Sikhs, along with us reverent or bemused scholars of religion, were caught up in a unity that went beyond our own intentions or expectations. The resonance of the responses by the great congregation became, for me, a perception of the Holy. For a moment, the place was no longer strange nor the words unfamiliar. They had become transparent in a moment of divine self-manifestation. The arguments and contention that had plagued our deliberations in the seminar melted away in the presence of the Holy where we were no longer strangers. Human words gave witness to the divine Word in a way for which our scholarly deliberations had not prepared us. God, the "Impressive Other," had broken through the limits of this experience to authenticate the divine presence.

Later, as we were being trundled back to the guest house, an inevitable question began to intrude into my consciousness. There had been, for me, an undeniable realization of God's presence at the Golden Temple. Yet how was this to be related to my personal confession that I had seen "the light of the knowledge of the glory of God in the face of Christ" (2 Cor. 4:6)? As the strangeness of the setting and the unfamiliarity of the words melted away, I had been brought face to face with a mystery. How could the God of Abraham, Isaac, and Jacob, the God and Father of our Lord Jesus Christ, be in this place where God was not known by the names I knew God by? But even more difficult was the question, how could I hold to faith in the absoluteness of Jesus Christ as Lord and yet believe that God had offered self-disclosure in this place where the name of Jesus is not even a whisper?

The Rejection of the Question

For some, my questions about religious pluralism and the Lordship of Christ have no real meaning or urgency. For fundamentalists, evangelical pietists, or adherents to scholastic orthodoxy, in either its Protestant or Roman Catholic versions, religious pluralism does not demand theological reformulation or a redirection of piety. Religious conservatives, old and new, argue that since Christianity demands an exclusive faith in Jesus Christ, it precludes any such question. The awareness of religious pluralism, for them, is an occasion for seeing the full scope of what Christian evangelism still has to do. My claims to an encounter with the Holy at the Golden Temple in Amritsar can be explained, or perhaps more accurately, explained away.

Some would see me as the victim of a demonic deception. Their argument is simple and straightforward. No authentic encounter with God exists save through the name of Jesus. All other supposed disclosures of the Holy are spurious, means by which the unwary are misled by the demonic. Did not Paul warn that "Satan disguises himself as an angel of light" (2 Cor. 11:14)? Others, wanting a more sophisticated explanation, would see me as the victim of self-deception. Was I not, after all, in the position of being an overly appreciative guest who too readily and uncritically identified with the values and ideals of my host?

My own Barthian theological background, with its withering critique of religious experience and natural theologies, would also reject my questions. As Barth argued so persuasively, Jesus Christ is known as the revelation of God only through the work of the Holy

Spirit and the witness of Scripture. Nothing outside this circle can be called a disclosure of God. No revelation is to be found there but only religion, and religion itself is the denial of revelation. For Barth, religion is "man's attempts to justify and to sanctify himself before a capricious and arbitrary picture of God."[2] Religion may have its depths, mysteries, and moments of profound insight and awareness, but, at most, religion can only show the depth and mysteries of the created order, for that is all human beings, even religious human beings, are capable of knowing outside of revelation.

Still others, equally bemused by my persistent problems with religious pluralism, are the anthropologists and historians of religion who see religious pluralism as the inevitable expression of the relativity of all cultures and ideologies. Different cultures have different religions. It is as simple as that. No amount of argumentation, the cultural relativist claims, can ever establish the finality of one religion over all others. God speaks in different ways to different peoples. A certain specificity about human perceptions of the Holy leads necessarily to religious pluralism. Human perceptions of the transcendent reflect the intellectual, emotional, esthetic, and moral values of the time and place in which they are made. In this light, religious pluralism is not problematic, it is the natural outcome of human particularity.

The Question Persistent Still

The difficulty with the various rejections of my questions about religious pluralism and the Lordship of Jesus is that they tend to falsify my experience at the Golden Temple. Neither the exclusivist nor the relativist deals with my experience on its own terms. But even more important, both the exclusivist and the relativist postions clash decisively with basic elements of Christian faith.

Christian exclusivism claims that its view of non-Christian religions is the only acceptable one because it grows directly from the Scripture, creeds, and confessions of the church. The evidence on their side is strong and cannot be lightly brushed aside. However, exclusivism is flawed at one vital point. While Christian claims for the Lordship of Jesus Christ are universal, Christianity itself is a particular religion in a world that is religiously plural and shows every sign of remaining so. At most Christians are less than one-third of the world's population. The majority of humankind has no way to hear the name of Jesus and respond to the Christian proclamation of his Lordship. Does this mean that in two-thirds of the world God is silent or known only in judgment?

If Jesus is Lord of all, then there must be some way in which his presence can be discerned in the whole world, including its religious traditions and cultures. Simply to withdraw huge sections of humankind from any possibility of salvation is a denial of the catholicity of the Christian faith. Christians have to take seriously the fact that God "did not leave himself without witness" (Acts 14:17). It is necessary to interpret exclusivist texts—"no one comes to the Father, but by me" (John 14:6)—in relation to texts of universal outlook—"For from the rising of the sun to its setting my name is great among the nations, and in every place incense is offered to my name, and a pure offering; for my name is great among the nations, says the LORD of hosts" (Mal. 1:11).

The dogmatic forms of Christian exclusivism are also flawed ethically. To condemn the vast majority of humankind to eternal perdition simply because they have had no chance to hear and respond to the gospel of Christ is immoral. It makes the Savior Lord of all into a cult deity who will look with favor on only a minority of the people of the world. To condemn people for what is, after all, only an accident of birth is to forget the words of the Apostle Peter, "Truly I perceive that God shows no partiality, but in every nation any one who fears him and does what is right is acceptable to him" (Acts 10:34–35). Any form of Christian exclusivism that denies people access to the grace of God because they were born into a Chinese commune, an Arabian village, a Russian collective farm, or an African tribe where no Christian proclamation is heard, renders God guilty of injustice. Christian exclusivism misunderstands the divine election of humankind in Jesus Christ. The word of Scripture at this point is clear: "For as in Adam all die, so also in Christ shall all be made alive" (1 Cor. 15:22). The text does not say, "As in Adam *all* die, so also in Christ shall *some* be made alive." As difficult as it may be for theology to conceptualize universal accessibility of the grace of God, this must be affirmed. If the grace of God is not universally accessible, then God is guilty of an unjust particularism.

What is being affirmed here is belief in universal access to God's grace. This is not to be confused with an uncritical universalism that affirms that all people are saved. Affirming the ultimate salvation of everyone is a speculative doctrine that goes beyond the evidence of Scripture. God alone is the Judge. The eternal destiny of all people is shrouded in the mystery of God's judgment (Rom. 11:33–34). The task of the church is to witness to the grace of God in Jesus. But the church does not have the task of judging human responses to that witness.

What is at issue is the universal availability of salvation. For Christian theology to affirm the Lordship of God over all, it must affirm universal access to the grace of God. The affirmation of the universal availability of this grace must be interpreted in relation to the obvious and continuing religious pluralism of the world. When the church confesses that in Jesus Christ, God has said "yes" to all people, it, of necessity, must include those who live out of other religious traditions or secular philosophies. Christian theology has had great difficulty in making this clear. Theologians have spoken of "extraordinary means of grace" that operate beyond the confines of the visible church. Augustine, Calvin, and the theologians of predestination all teach that the elect, the whole people of God, is not identical with the visible church. There are nonelect within the visible church and elect outside it. Yet these are, at best, peripheral and grudging ways of dealing with the problem. What is needed is a full and frank analysis of the ways in which God is present and gracious to the whole world. Without this vision the church is condemned to reiterate those distorting forms of particularism that have plagued its relationship to the rest of the world for so long.

Religious Relativism

Religious relativism is also critically flawed. When examined closely, it dies the death of a thousand qualifications. Human religiousness is a complex and contradictory phenomenon that cannot be dealt with by the easy assurance that God speaks in different ways to different people. Religions make claims for one God, many gods, or even no god at all. Religious traditions hold to ethical norms of universal benevolence and of particularistic exclusivism. Cultic demands range from a simple morality to complex magical rituals. Religious beliefs may deepen and enhance human life or threaten and destroy it. Religious language points to realities immanent or transcendent, past or future, exclusive or inclusive. Religious traditions do not point to a single level of reality, nor do they seem to converge. Amid these contradictions, religious relativism disintegrates into confusion.

To imply that all religions have a basis in some deep underlying ground of being does not solve the problem of religious relativism. The contradictory teachings and values found in the history of religions cannot be attributed to some reality called "God" and still give that word any self-consistent meaning. Mystical and idealistic philosophies seek to overcome the problem of religious relativism by thinking of the Holy as beyond all names and forms, but to relate the experience of the Holy to an undifferentiated "something" provides no grounds for intellectual or ethical discernment.

This lack of discernment clashes with the Christian understanding of revelation. Christians profess a faith in the one God who is self-revealing. God makes the divine name known so that people may call on God (Exod. 3:13–22). Revelation makes possible ethical and intellectual discourse about God's will and way in the world. The Christian understanding of revelation implies a pattern of meaning by which the presence of God may be discerned.

The early church was aware of the need for discernment in its struggle with religious pluralism, not only in the pagan world that surrounded it but also within the community of faith itself. Some means had to be found to "test the spirits to see whether they are of God." The norm by which the Christian community discerns the presence and activity of God in the world is Christological. As the early church put it, "every spirit which confesses that Jesus Christ has come in the flesh is of God" (1 John 4:1–2). The question before the Christian community today is, whether discerning judgments can be made about religious traditions without falling into destructive, self-righteous exclusivism.

The Christian "Between a Rock and a Hard Place"

Christians have great difficulty thinking in an even-handed way about other religious traditions and the claims made for them as pointing to sources of salvation. Awareness of other religions has been one of ignorance, angry rejection, or at best grudging acceptance. The tragic history of the Crusades, pogroms, the Holocaust, and assorted holy wars mounted in the name of Christ is a scandal the church cannot ignore. In a world threatened by nuclear weapons there is no room left for destructive exclusivism.

Christian exclusivism came into existence for a host of reasons. At times, this exclusivism has reflected the cultural imperialism and arrogance of Western civilization in its conquests of the Third World. At other times, destructive exclusivism has come from the misplaced zeal of the religious fanatic who brooks no opposition, but the problem of Christian exclusivism cannot be written off with *ad hominem* arguments. To explain the difficulties Christians have had with other religious traditions only in terms of arrogance and ill will is to miss what is vital. Christians have feared that any but a negative view of other religions would be unfaithful to Jesus Christ. Any compromise would undercut loyalty to Jesus as Lord and, hence, endanger the salvation that comes through him alone. The Christian community remembers its martyr saints down through the centuries from Stephen to Oscar Romero. They gave up life itself to defend their faith in Jesus Christ against the demonic claims of other lords. To ignore this dimension of Christianity in the search for a new and wider vision is not a possibility.

Evangelical conservatives have been right in their rejection of liberal attempts to overcome Christian exclusivism. The ethical idealism of William Ernest Hocking (1873–1966) in *The Laymen's Report on Foreign Missions* was offered as the way in which to reinterpret all religions as men and women search for understanding and deeper community. Arnold Toynbee (1889–1975) held out the promise of a religion of the future that would combine the best features of Christianity with Buddhism and Hinduism, while rejecting the particularism of Judaism and Islam. The difficulty with these approaches is that they reduce all religions to the level of what is acceptable to a liberal-humanistic philosophy. They do not deal with religious traditions as they are self-defined but in terms of the philosopher's own philosophy. What is needed is a way to relate positively to the religions of the world that grows out of the Christian commitment to Jesus Christ. There is no point in ex-Christians trying to relate to ex-Hindus, ex-Buddhists, or ex-Muslims. What we need is a way of being faithful to Jesus Christ as Lord that does not denigrate other religious options. The place to start is with an analysis of how religious communities recognize and respond to the transcendent.

Being Finite and Being Faithful

Human beings are finite although we live amid intimations of the infinite. To be human is to live on the boundary between what we make, shape, and control and that which makes, shapes, and controls us. We know that we are limited and that death is the destiny of all humans. Amid our lives we struggle against meaninglessness, guilt, and despair. Yet at the same time, we are lured by the awareness of the fulfillment of human life. We look for sources of hope and joy that transcend where we now are. We dream of the transformation of our threatened existence into a life abundant and eternal. On this boundary, we search for a faith that will allow us to live in hope amid the tragedy and chaos of everyday life.

The religious traditions of humankind offer a means for orienting human life along this boundary between life and death. As finite people, hemmed in by death and the sheer chanciness of life, we seek a faith that will point us to sources of hope that transcend us. Through our religious traditions humans seek a faith that will link the believer to the transcendent. Just here, however, is the paradox of the human religious search. While what we seek in faith is the transcendent with its promise of infinite fulfillment, we are shaped religiously by our loyalties to particular people, values, and institutions. As humans we do not have the ability to leap out of our own skins, as it were, to some lofty vantage point from which to judge the truth claims of the various religions. Judgments about religious ideas, institutions, or values are based on knowledge of the various religions. Our perceptions of other religions are given their distinctive character by our own faith commitments. Hence, all reflection on religious pluralism is inevitably confessional. It arises out of our personal history and that of the religious community of which we are a part.

The Starting Point for Christians

The starting point for the Christian community in reflecting on other religions is the revelation of God in Jesus. This revelation has two aspects. On the one hand, the revelation of God in Jesus is concrete and personal. Knowledge of God and salvation is tied to the life, death, and resurrection of a particular person, Jesus of Nazareth, who lived in a definite time and place, "under Pontius Pilate." The community that has received Jesus as revelation, the Christian Church, is a particular religious community. Christianity, the religion reared in the name of Jesus, is a religion among the religions of the world. *The Confession of 1967* (PCUSA) includes in its confession of Christian faith the place of Christianity among the religions of the world:

> The church in its mission encounters the religions of men and in that encounter becomes conscious of its own human character as a religion. . . . The Christian finds parallels between other religions and his own and must approach all religions with openness and respect (2.A.3).

On the other hand, what is revealed in Jesus and celebrated by the church is nothing less than the revelation of God the Lord of all. Jesus Christ has established a universal covenant that embraces all peoples. Jesus has promised the kingdom of God which will be the outcome of the judging and redeeming work of God with the whole world. As H. Richard Niebuhr (1894–1962) analyzed the Christian confession of revelation in Jesus, it implies more than an understanding of Jesus. Jesus Christ is "the special occasion" to which the church looks to see "the righteousness of God, his power and wisdom. But from that special occasion we also derive the concepts which make possible the elucidation of all events in our history."[3] Hence, the revelation in Jesus is universal and forms the basis for understanding not only the church but other religious communities as well. The problem facing the church today is how to relate the particular historical ways in which it has received revelation to the universal claim it makes that its proclamation witnesses to God the Lord. There must be a way for Christians to remain faithful in their commitment to Jesus Christ without falling into destructive exclusivism or indifferent syncretism.

7

Faith in Jesus Christ

The Meaning of Miracles

Talk about miracles makes many Christians today uneasy. Since the eighteenth century, Christians have tried, with indifferent success, to relate the miracle stories of Scripture and tradition to the new scientific worldview that has so dominated Western civilization. Whether by a rigid insistence on their historicity or by efforts to explain them away, miracles have created far more heat than light for modern theology. Thus it would seem folly to seek to resolve one vexed question—the universality of salvation in Christ—by an equally vexed problem—miracles. Yet the two belong together, for it is through miracle that religious communities recognize and respond to revelation. The pattern of how religious people and communities identify certain events and persons as a disclosure of the Holy has two elements: (1) the miracle itself, and (2) its ecstatic reception as revelation.[1]

(1) The Miracle

"Miracle" is the name given by religious traditions to those persons or events through which there is an encounter with the Holy. A miracle points to the transcendent because it is an event that goes beyond what people expect to happen. Miracles are not magic tricks, nor are they events that break the supposedly "immutable laws of science." They are what David Tracy calls "limit experiences."[2] A miracle goes beyond what people ordinarily think should happen. It points to powers and possibilities that transcend ordinary, everyday encounters with the world and the people in it.

Human life has a kind of texture about it. We expect to go to work on Monday morning, we expect our cars to start, we expect love from our spouses, we expect help from our friends. We know that not all of these things always happen. Yet when they do happen they are not a surprise. They are within the limits of what we ordinarily expect. Then there are events in life that go beyond the usual. There is healing where ordinarily we would expect illness and death. There is enlightenment where only blinding ignorance had held sway. There is resurrection where death had destroyed the last possibility of renewal. When we encounter one of these limit experiences, we start to ask questions. Why did this happen? What new powers caused this? What new possibilities does this event create for the future? A miracle is an event powerful enough to create wonder. A miracle is an event strong enough to cause people to react to it and make decisions about it. The history of religions is replete with such events.

The young prince Siddhartha (c. 563–c. 483 B.C.) exhausts the resources of spiritual teachers and the pathway of asceticism in his search for enlightenment. Only then does he reach enlightenment and become the Buddha. The unlettered prophet Mohammad (c. 570–632) dictates to his followers the eloquent poetry of the Qur'an. Moses flees Egypt after his abortive attempt to be a freedom fighter for his people, when he is confronted by Yahweh in the burning bush. Guru Nanak returns after everyone thought he had drowned in the River Bein to announce his gospel of reconciliation that had been given to him by the Eternal. The normal pattern of expectations was broken.

Miracles are not trivial events, nor simply peculiar, inexplicable happenings. They are emotionally and intellectually compelling events. They have the power to make other events intelligible because they point to sources of meaning and hope that go beyond the particular event itself. They are important not only for the persons caught up in the event but for others because miracles are events that reveal a way of salvation.

(2) Ecstatic Reception

The reception of miracles as revelation is an act of ecstatic response. With its reception, the miracle discloses the divine to a community of faith. To call the reception of a miracle as revelation "ecstatic" does not imply a highly charged emotional state. This may or may not be part of the response of the community at any given time. The reception of an event or person as revelation goes beyond the ways in which people usually think or feel about the world. Ecstatic reception means that "flesh and blood has not revealed this to you, but my Father who is in heaven" (Matt. 16:17). It is received because of the inner testimony of the Holy Spirit. Or as the Sikh community confesses in its prayer, the *Japuji*, "God is the Enlightener, and can be realized by grace of himself alone."

The ecstatic reception of an event or person as revelation goes beyond the norms for rationality, yet it is not irrational. The miracle as a saving revelation discloses new patterns of rationality. Those who do not accept a miracle as revelation must make some alternate explanation for what has happened. One of the most common ways to reject a miracle is to claim that it is a deception or an evidence of insanity. Jesus' sanity was doubted by his own family (Mark 3:21). Paul was thought mad by Festus (Acts 26:24). Guru Nanak's parents called a physician to cure him of his peculiar silences and strange talk. The opponents of Mohammad accused him of deception and of bending God's word to his own will.

The ecstatic reception of miracles is affectively strong, but emotional intensity does not validate it. The reception of a miracle as revelation is validated by its power to bring new being. It discloses a source of salvation. A miracle is an event that demands a response; it cannot be ignored. Yet the response of faith always has an element of risk in it. A leap of faith is necessary for a particular person or event to be taken as the center of meaning and hope. The believer exercises an element of choice in opting for salvation through ways not accepted by everyone else.

What we propose then is to examine the ways in which the Christian community receives Jesus, his life, death, and resurrection, as the disclosure of salvation. Such an analysis can give some clues as to how the Christian community can perceive itself in relation to the other religious communities of the world.

Christians and Miracles

Since the eighteenth century, Christians have had a kind of love-hate relationship to miracles. Conservative Protestant theology has had two approaches to miracles. It has affirmed the historicity of the miracles of Jesus and the primitive church, while using historical criticism to reject the miracles reported by other religious traditions. By doing this, Christians hoped to preserve their own faith while undercutting the claims of other religions. This was a shrewd apologetic move, in many ways. Such a line of argument allowed Christians to identify with the scientific world view that rejected miracles. They could join the rationalists in heaping scorn on the miracle stories of pagan and Jewish antiquity. Protestants could reject miracles claimed by Catholics as spurious and so establish the rational superiority of their religion. As miracle stories from Hinduism, Buddhism, Islam, and the primal religious traditions became known, they too were rejected as fraud or illusion. This apologetic greatly reduced but never eliminated the miraculous. The miracles of Jesus and those of the so-called "age of revelation" were retained as historical. All else was rejected by rationalistic, scientific criticism.

The difficulty with this line of argumentation soon became evident. There is no way in which the originating events of Christianity could be exempted from the same criticism as that used against other faiths. The rejection of the miracles of the rivals of Christianity, both ancient and modern, was the prelude to the rejection of the miracles of Jesus and primitive Christianity. David Hume (1711–76) saw that the logic of the rationalistic apologists for Christianity such as Bishop John Tillotson (1630–94) could be extended to level the very religion that was being defended.[3] Historical criticism and scientific explanation could not be used selectively against some miracle stories while exempting others. Because of this, modern theological conservatism has been driven to insist upon the historicity of the biblical miracles as a matter of faith. The historicity of miracles is to be accepted on the authority of Scripture. The difficulty here is that the argument from author-

ity negates the miracle apologetic as a means for authenticating the
Christian claim to revelation.

By contrast to this theological conservatism, modernist and liberal theologies accepted scientific and historical criticism of the miracle stories. Their apologetics rejected historical miracles as the
guarantors of Christian revelation but accepted in their place the
subjective miracles of conversion. The validation of the Christian
revelation was the power of Jesus and his teachings to change the
consciousness of those who had faith in him. The pattern of this
apologetic was set by Schleiermacher who argued that the highest
form of communion with God is that of the Christian. Such communion with God is, however, available in "no other way . . . than
through faith in Jesus as the Redeemer."[4] The verification of revelation in Jesus is in his unique power to incorporate humankind into a
fuller God-consciousness. This power establishes the absoluteness of
Christianity. Modern theology has since worked many variations on
this line of argumentation. In contemporary terms, a chastened form
is found in existentialist theologies that argue from the unique power
of the kerygma, the Christian proclamation of Jesus, to bring about
the transition from inauthentic to authentic existence.[5]

While less dogmatically certain than the conservatives, liberal
theology was confident of the superiority of Christianity. Christianity, according to the liberals, was the inner core of the superior
culture of the Western world which was, by the end of the nineteenth
century, thought to be replacing that of other religions and cultures
all over the world. Yet the difficulties with an apologetic based on
the interior miracle of conversion also soon became evident. Eventually, other religions—Buddhism was a favorite candidate—were recognized as having a message of love that made them comparable to
Christianity.[6] They too could speak of conversion to higher forms of
consciousness. However, most liberals and modernists retained their
confidence in the absoluteness of Christianity. They saw Christianity
as the disclosure of what is essential in all human religiousness.
Christianity was not simply a religion among others; it was the quin-
tessential religion of humankind. Personal faith in Jesus empowered
living by the most noble ethic and the deepest possible communion
with God.

The limits of this confidence, in either its liberal or conservative form, became evident when Ernst Troeltsch explored critically the arguments for the absoluteness of Christianity used in modern theology. Troeltsch concluded that historical and philosophical reflection could only establish the "relative absoluteness" of a particular religion for its own cultural group and time in history. However, this does not destroy the importance of Christianity for us, he maintained. We may claim truth for ourselves without being able to prove that what we receive as revelation is universally true. Near the end of his life, Troeltsch concluded his reflection on the relationship of Christianity to other religions by saying, "I hope you feel that I am not speaking in any spirit of skepticism or uncertainty. A truth which, in the first instance, is *a truth for us* does not cease, because of this, to be very Truth and Life."[7] It is impossible to establish the finality of Jesus as absolute revelation for all people in all times. Yet a personal faith in Jesus as the disclosure of God is a possibility for Troeltsch.

By early in the nineteenth century, the conservative apologetic from Jesus' miracles had been reduced to an argument from authority. By early in the twentieth century, the liberal apologetic from the interior miracle of conversion was reduced to redundancy. To have faith in Jesus was to express a preference, but this preference could claim no validation save the deep conviction of the believer. The result has been that the miracles of Jesus have been deprived of any function in informing our faith in him.

Another Option on Miracles

A different approach to miracles was taken by the early church as it proclaimed and defended its faith in Jesus. The argument was not between Christians who accepted the historicity of his miracles and their Jewish or pagan opponents who denied their historical character. Both friends and foes of early Christianity accepted the historicity of Jesus' miracles. Their questions were of a different sort from those asked today. Their concern was with the nature of the forces at work in the miracles. Their questions were about what forces, natural or supernatural, benevolent or malevolent, were revealed in the miracles. Christians understood Jesus' miracles as evidence of the near approach of the kingdom of God and the resurrection as his vindication by God the Father. Opponents of Christianity understood his miracles as products of his powers as a magician or his ability to utilize malevolent powers, while his resurrection was a fraud.[8] For the Christians there was a correlation between the miracle, which is a historical event, and its reception as revelation. For the non-Christians there was no such correlation. To be sure, for Christian and non-Christian alike, the miracle was an event that broke with the usual expectations of what could happen, but it remained for the non-Christian only an extraordinary event that had to be fitted into some existing scheme of explanation.

Human religiousness is characterized by miracles because "religion is always directed towards salvation, never towards life itself as it is given."[9] Religion, by its very nature, is perceived through miracles. Gerhard van der Leeuw shows religion to be concerned with "a *highly exceptional* and *extremely impressive 'Other'* " that obtrudes into human experience and gives rise to feelings of amazement. The power of this *impressive Other* "becomes authenticated in things and persons, and by virtue of which these are influential and effective."[10] The miracle is the disclosure of the *"impressive Other"* that disrupts the texture of life and raises the question of what new powers and possibilities are at work. In the reports of miracles there are legendary accretions, misperceptions, and even elements of fraud, yet miracles cannot be reduced to these. Their historicity is in their power to go beyond the limits of existence, as it is now known, to create new opportunities for human life. As such, miracles are open to investigation that can disclose the structures of being implicit in them.

The early church did not distinguish, as has modern theology, between the "inner" miracle of conversion and the so-called "outer" miracles involving healing, feeding, or power over natural forces. In the Gospels, both inner and outer miracles are blended in a way that has been the vexation of modern historians. The authority of Jesus that gave power to his teachings was the same power he showed over demons or illness (for example, Mark 1:21–28). There was no notion here of human beings existing in a closed world in which God is only able to change human consciousness or promote new ethical values.

The "inside-outside" distinction was not a factor in early Christian thought because they believed the world to be open to transcendent forces, both benevolent and malevolent, on all levels. The miracle raises questions because it breaks with the expectations people have for a particular situation. The sick are made well, the corrupt become pure, the blind see, the lame walk, sinners repent. These events point beyond themselves. The normal expectation would be that sick people die, corrupt people become more greedy, the blind are left groping in darkness, and the sinner deepens in depravity. When the usual does not occur, there is a perception of some extraordinary power or powers at work.

When Jesus healed a dumb demoniac, "all the people were amazed and said, 'Can this be the Son of David?' But when the Pharisees heard it they said, 'It is only by Beelzebul, the prince of demons, that this man casts out demons' " (Matt. 12:22–24). As this story makes clear, the miracle did not do away with the need for faith. It does not prove the divinity of Jesus. The miracle makes the question of his divinity possible. It raises the question, Is this person "the Son of David," that is, the messianic deliverer sent by God, or is he the agent of the demons? There had been a break in the texture of life. What was thought to be inevitable had not happened. Such an event calls for a response: faith in Jesus as the revelation of God was the response of the Christians. The miracle did not remove the need for faith by serving as a proof. Instead, the miracle raised the question of faith by pointing beyond itself to the power at work in it.

The reception of a miracle as revelation by faith does not create the historicity of that event. Faith is a reaction to its historicity. The ecstatic reception of an event as revelation acknowledges an "*impressive Other*" at work in the event. But the reception by faith involves more than that. The reception of one event as revelation involves the affirmation of the power of that event or person to illumine the meaning of other events and persons. When an event is claimed to be revelatory, it brings not disinterested information about the Beyond but saving truth. How does this analysis relate to the way in which the Christian community has received the resurrection of Jesus?

The history of religions contains accounts of disappearing bodies and visions of the deceased that purportedly have universal significance and have given rise to religious movements.[11] As in the case of the resurrection of Jesus, the explanations of such phenomena given by members of religious communities may well be as likely as any given by critical historians. In each case, it is possible to point to some form of historical evidence. There has been a break in the texture of everyday life. There is no historical evidence, however, to establish any one of these events as the key to the meaning of all human affairs. Yet it is just this that Christians affirm about Jesus' resurrection. Christians see in Jesus' resurrection the key to all history because it is valued as the unique discernment point for knowing God. While faith does not establish its historicity, faith does select a particular event as the key for understanding everything else. Historical knowledge by its very nature cannot do that. Historical knowledge springs from the human ability to comprehend the world. Faith is an act of human freedom to be related to that which transcends the world through an event accepted as revelation. Faith is an act of human selftranscendence to select one event from a number of possible events as the discernment point for finding the meaning of all that is.

The starting point for evaluating the claims of Christian faith is not the rejection of miracles in all other traditions. Every religious tradition has its origins and its history characterized by events that break with the normal pattern of expectations. Faith is the response that chooses certain of these events as the disclosure of ultimate reality. In the Christian tradition, faith in Jesus Christ discloses the pattern of God's saving activity in the whole world. To understand that disclosure it is necessary first to reflect on two facts. First, there is a plurality of religious options given in the world. Second, the world is open to the emergence of novelty.

Religious Pluralism and an Open World

Some basic changes have occurred in contemporary science and philosophy that allow a new interpretation of miracles.

The first is the collapse in modern scientific research of the myth of the "ghost in the machine."[12] It is no longer possible to conceive of human life as the combination of the mind or soul, which is open to change, existing in a body and world which is fully determined by mechanistic law. The mind and body interpenetrate one another. Although human beings transcend the natural order, they exist in and through it. The world cannot be conceived as fully determined, while the human mind or consciousness alone is open to change by an act of faith or will. Instead, human existence goes on in a world of which it is an integral part. But this world is not fully determined like a vast clockwork mechanism. To be sure, there are patterns of expectation that characterize our understanding of ourselves and the world. Human behavior and the natural order are not random or chaotic. These patterns of expectation are expressed scientifically, not as rigid laws, but as statistical norms. The world is a mixture of order and contingency that cannot be reduced to rigid determinism. Hence a miracle is not God's decision to break the natural law to make the Godhead known.[13] Rather, there is openness in the self and in the world that allows new events to emerge. These events, viewed religiously as miracles, may be received ecstatically as revelation through which faith emerges for an individual or a community.

The second factor shaping a new approach to miracles is the awareness of religious pluralism. The question of faith must be dealt with in light of the variety of alternatives found in different religious traditions. The decision of faith is not limited to the choice between Christianity or some secular philosophy of life. A variety of options are now open by other traditions. The question of faith in Jesus Christ has to be approached in relation to them. The history of religions provides the means for locating and articulating the character of Christianity in relation to other religious alternatives.

The miracles of a particular religious tradition contain its understanding of new being and the means for obtaining it. The nature and source of salvation are given in the events a community of faith receives as miracles. Hence, miracles are moments of high seriousness. They are not prodigies to be done for amusement, as Jesus' refusal of Herod's plea to have a miracle performed for his amusement (Luke 23:6–16). The miracle has an implicit claim in it about new being.

The potency of miracles varies greatly. Some are perception

events that give rise to whole new religious communities and form comprehensive modes of self and world understanding. The potency of other miracles extends to only a few people or, perhaps, a single individual, giving the possibility of a new faith orientation. Some miracles are of high valency. They bring many elements of human existence into new order and give birth to massive religious communities. Others have low valency and touch only a few aspects of human life. The common element in the miracle is its ability to point beyond itself. When the church received Jesus' resurrection, it declared it to be a miracle of the highest valency because it embraced life on all levels. His resurrection is "the resurrection of the body," not merely the persistence of the soul.

The Ambiguity of Miracles

Miracles, no more than the religious traditions of which they are a part, are not exempt from judgment. Miracles may point to destructive powers. The demonic has power to break through our pattern of expectations to point to the negative trying to make itself absolute. This is why the primitive Christian community was so concerned with discerning the source of the spiritual forces at work in its midst. The ecstasy and miraculous powers associated with the demonic were real, as no one in the early church denied (1 Cor. 12:1–3; Acts 19:11–20). The problem was how to find the miracles that point to the creative and renewing power of God rather than to the demonic. What was needed was a canon, "a measuring stick" (Gk. *kanon*), by which to determine the source and meaning of claims to new spiritual power. The primitive church used the life, death, and resurrection of Jesus Christ as its canon. However, the mere mention of the name of Jesus was not sufficient because the name could be misused (Matt. 12:30; Acts 19:13). The name had to be defined or it could be used as a magical password, as in Gnosticism. The name of Jesus was defined through his life, death, and resurrection (1 John 4:1–3; 1 Cor. 2:2). When the name is given its proper definition, it discloses new being and makes possible discernment of the presence of God in the world.

The problem of discernment among miracles is the source of the strange alternation in the New Testament between the inclusive and the exclusive use of the name of Jesus. On the one hand, Jesus says of an exorcist who used his name, "For he that is not against us is for us" (Mark 9:39). On the other hand, he is reported as saying, "He who is not with me is against me" (Matt. 12:30). This alternation reflects the struggle to define the name of Jesus. On the one hand, the power of new being in the name of Jesus extends beyond the confines of his immediate followers. The powers of the kingdom to which Jesus witnesses are universal. Wherever there is victory over the enslaving powers of the demonic, the power of God, as disclosed by Jesus, is at work. On the other hand, the early church realized that the name of Jesus could be manipulated as a means of self-seeking gain (Acts 19:11–20). When the name of Jesus is used in that way, it does not bring release from the demonic powers. The exorcist by manipulating the name of Jesus refuses himself to come under the power of Jesus. It is necessary to come under the judgment of Jesus in order to receive grace through him. Hence, "He who is not with me is against me."

The outcome of this controversy became clear within the first few generations of the life of the church. The name of Jesus provides a canon for discerning and participating in the power of new being only as it is defined through his life, death, and resurrection. The name of Jesus is not an arbitrary verbalism but the codification of the means of salvation. The name of Jesus codifies the way to salvation through death and resurrection. The task of theology is to explicate this name afresh in light of the new circumstances in which the Christian community finds itself today.

Faith in Jesus

To place the question of faith in Jesus in the context of religious pluralism cancels the apologetic stance of granting reality to the miracles of Jesus while denying it to all others. Religions are characterized by miracles that disclose the claims each one makes about new being and human access to it. It is impossible to look from the outside at these miracles and prove that one is inherently superior to the other. It is impossible to argue that Christian miracles are superior to Buddhist ones, or that Sufi miracles are higher than Hindu ones. Historically viewed, miracles set forth different visions of the fulfillment of human life in relation to that which transcends it. When a particular miracle is received ecstatically by an individual or community through faith, it receives absoluteness. It becomes the definitive pattern for participation in the Holy for that person or community.

The miracle is the break in the pattern of expectations that calls forth faith, but faith is an act of commitment. Faith involves a leap. It is an act of ecstasy—standing outside one's self. In faith a person makes a choice despite the ambiguity of all human decisions. The specific faith of the Christian is the acceptance of the salvation in Jesus Christ opened through his life, death, and resurrection. To choose to live by faith in Jesus is to accept his disclosure of new life and the human future as coming from God. It is, from our perspective, to grant Christ absoluteness. To have this faith is to affirm that his vision is real and not a chimera. However, to have the faith of the church in Jesus does not necessitate rejection of new being except as found through participation in some visible Christian community.

Faith in Jesus Christ is not faith in a tribal god but the universal Lord. The Christian may be open to reality as disclosed in other religions and their miraculous disclosure events. But this openness is not uncritical. In dialogue with those living by other religious traditions, Christians discern truth in them because of what is known through Jesus. Dialogue with other religions does not mean the abandonment of the commitment the Christian makes to Jesus. Dialogue is the means for realizing the universality of the revelation in him. Faith in Jesus Christ utilizes the vision of new life given in Christ as the norm for affirming and sharing in God's creative and redemptive presence wherever it is found in the world.

The Encoding of New Being

The salvation granted in the life, death, and resurrection of Jesus is distorted if it is not received in its totality. Resurrection does not stand alone as the source and pattern of new life. Resurrection must always be related to crucifixion. There is a dialectic to salvation in Jesus Christ that is broken by separating the resurrection from the crucifixion. The dialectic is the movement from judgment to redemption and was revealed by Jesus in his own life, death, and resurrection. The new life of the disciple recapitulates Jesus' own movement from crucifixion to resurrection (Gal. 2:20; Rom. 6:5–11). The new being in Christ is not simply the infinite extension of human powers as they now exist. In other words, salvation is not through resurrection without crucifixion. Human moral, intellectual, emotional, and spiritual capacities are created by God, but they are now under the power of sin. The exertion of these human capacities in their present distorted state inevitably falls into contradiction. To use the Pauline terminology, this is what happens when humans seek salvation through "works righteousness." In their present distorted state all human powers must come under judgment. They are subject to death.

In the dialectic of salvation in Christ, the old centers of security must be surrendered in death to self in order to move toward the resurrection of new being. Salvation means a shift from seeking security in human powers, what we make and control, to life in God, whom humans cannot make or control. In Jesus' words, "Whoever seeks to gain his life will lose it, but whoever loses his life will preserve it" (Luke 17:33). This is what happens when humankind finds salvation in "the righteousness of faith," as Paul called it, or "justification."

Salvation in Christ has a pattern or form. When this pattern is known, it becomes possible to discern its presence in the whole world. The salvation empowered by Jesus is at work wherever the dialectic of judgment and redemption, death and resurrection is found. By knowing the pattern of new being in Christ, it becomes possible to relate Christian revelation to other religions. Two aspects of the new being in Christ provide clues for discerning and affirming the presence of God in the world.

First, salvation in Christ is inclusive. It embraces all levels of existence. Hence, salvation is in the transformation of the created order and the self, not their destruction or a flight from them.

Second, salvation is in the dialectic of death and resurrection. Salvation is not in the infinite extension of human powers because they are now distorted by sin. Paradoxically, it is only when these powers are abandoned in repentance that new being emerges in divine judgment and renewal.

What has been encountered in Jesus may be said to be "the encoding of new being." His life, death, and resurrection define the pattern of communal and personal growth in the new life. They also do more than define this new life. They are its empowerment. This is what Christians mean in their confession of the divinity of Christ. What was revealed in Jesus discloses the fundamental power of God at work in the universe. "In Christ *God* was reconciling the world to himself" (2 Cor. 5:19). Yet the absoluteness of revelation in Jesus does not mean that salvation is found only amid the community of Christians. This absoluteness is grounded in the saving movement from death to resurrection, judgment to redemption, self-abnegation to self-fulfillment as the pathway to salvation. It is a pathway created by God.

The metaphor of "encoding" is used here to express the scope of new being in Jesus Christ. "Encoding" takes its definition from the science of genetics. Genes are those units of life that provide, through the structure of their DNA molecules, the basic patterns by which a being assimilates the materials and forces that surround it in its own distinctive way. The gene encodes the distinctive forms and functions of a plant, animal, fish, or bird. Apple trees produce apples and not pears; baby lions become grown lions and do not turn into elephants in the process. Genetic encoding is the storage of the information that directs the assimilation of materials into the distinctive structures of each kind of life. The structures of human life are maintained in their complex forms by patterns encoded in the genes. The genes are the key to the whole structure of a particular person, but are not themselves all there is to that structure. Genes have encoded the capacity to appropriate and integrate many and different forces and materials into one unique being.

The metaphor of encoding provides a model of how salvation in Jesus works. New being disclosed and empowered in Jesus has the capacity of structuring the whole of existence. Hence the pattern of new being encoded in Christ may potentially be encountered in other religious traditions. The "name of Jesus" encodes a power capable of assimilating elements from all cultures into its distinctive form of life. This power of new being, encoded in Jesus, is at work wherever men and women give up their present centers of security in trusting openness to the transcendent. Christians identify and live out of this pattern of new being because of what they know through conscious commitment to Jesus Christ. They know him through a religious tradition built in conscious relation to Christ's act of divine self-disclosure. Other religious traditions may live out of this power of new being in accordance with ways in which they encounter and participate in ultimate reality. This does not make them crypto-Christians or members of a "hidden" or "latent church."[14] They are and remain what they are—Hindus, Buddhists, Jews, Muslims, or devotees of a myriad of other religions. But at work within these religions may be that underlying pattern of new being disclosed and empowered by Jesus, the power of death and resurrection.

Christianity as a Religion

The encoding of new being in Jesus is both the critical and constructive principle by which Christians may live faithfully amid religious pluralism. The implications of this encoding of salvation in the name of Jesus may be seen in two ways.

First, it is impossible to say that God is only at work in and through Christianity. The absoluteness of what has been revealed in Jesus does not mean the absoluteness of the Christian religion. To claim such absoluteness for the Christian religion is to deny the universality of the Lordship of God. This is a danger that has always threatened the traditional understanding of other religions set forth in Cyprian's dictum, "Outside the church, no salvation."

Second, it is impossible to say that all religions are equally good and simply reflect differing conditions and capacities of humankind. Such an uncritical religious relativism denies the demonic tendencies in all religions. Danger is implicit in the well-meaning attempts to overcome the tensions that arise between religious communities with the assurance that ultimately all religions are the same.

A third possibility for witness and dialogue with other religions is open to Christians. The starting point for this becomes evident when

Christians recognize their own religious communities, their institutions, theologies, and traditions as a religion among the other religions. The Presbyterian Church, U.S.A., has given a unique confessional expression to this fact in its *Confession of 1967:*

> The church in its mission encounters the religions of men and in that encounter becomes conscious of its own human character as a religion.... The Christian religion, as distinct from God's revelation of himself, has been shaped throughout its history by the cultural forms of its environment (2.A.3).

While the revelation of God in Jesus Christ has absoluteness for Christian faith, the Christian religion that has developed in response to this revelation is not absolute. Christianity reflects not only the revelation in Jesus but also its reception in a variety of cultures and times. Christianity, just as other religions, is open to demonic distortions and must be brought under the judgment of Jesus Christ. This is the critical truth enshrined in the distinction Karl Barth made between revelation and religion. Religion is a human activity, even when it emerges in response to the revelatory events in Jesus Christ. Revelation apprehended by faith is God's gift, not a human accomplishment.

The limitation of Barth's position springs from his not taking the Christological norm and applying it to other religions as well.[15] If in Jesus there is encoded new being, the universal power for reconstituting human life, then this power may be perceived and shared by humankind in various religions. What is implied here is not the grudging admission that Christians have sometimes made for the possibility of salvation through "extraordinary means of grace," for those not in communion with the church. Rather, as Hans Küng (b. 1928) has pointed out, the non-Christian religions are "the ordinary means of grace" for the vast majority of humankind.[16]

The distinctiveness of Christianity lies in the way in which it carries through its Scripture, traditions, and institutions a witness to Jesus Christ. It is the community to which he is known personally. It is the community of witness. The Christian community has the responsibility of preserving the authenticity of its witness to the life, death, and resurrection of Jesus Christ.

To enter into dialogue with other religions is not to accept religious syncretism. Dialogue is a noncoercive witness to the freedom of God the Lord to be present in all parts of the world, even in religious traditions other than those of the church. By faithful interpretation of Scripture and critical judgments on its own ethical and intellectual life, the church seeks to clarify its witness to Jesus. However, this witness is given in the realization that God's action through Jesus Christ is universal in scope and not limited to the community that gives the witness. The universality of what God is doing in Jesus is not created by the church although the church witnesses to this universality by its words and deeds. The church is the community of witness and service which confesses God as made known through Christ. The church speaks in "the name of Jesus" against the sinful distortion of human life, and it speaks for renewal in the paradigm of death and resurrection. Yet this witness will only be effective when the word of judgment and redemption is spoken to Christianity as well as to other religions.

8

Jesus and
the Whole World

Universality in Time and Space

In interpreting Jesus through the traditions of Jewish eschatology, the early church encountered the problem of universality in its most acute form. Jesus was proclaimed Lord of all times and places. Jesus, who had appeared in history, was confessed as the source of the salvation promised before by the prophets. As eschatological Lord, his judgment and redemption embrace all people and places. Salvation in Christ is eschatological because it is final in both space and time. It is not to be one form of salvation among many. It is the only salvation. The early church was clear on this point. "And there is salvation in no else, for there is no other name under heaven given among men by which we must be saved" (Acts 4:12). That name is the name of Jesus confessed as Lord (Phil. 2:9–11). To see what this means today requires a look at some history.

First-century Judaism had a definite logic for relating the particularity of its religion to the universality of Yahweh. The Jews understood themselves to be a chosen people called by God to reveal divine law. This law is universal, as is the sovereignty of Yahweh. The sovereignty of Yahweh is not dependent on the political or religious triumph of Judaism. It is divine justice that causes the rise and fall of the nations, whether they recognize the power that shapes their destiny or not. At the end time, the revelation of God that has been entrusted to the Jews will be recognized by all nations who will then gather around Israel.

The exact way in which the nations were to be brought to recognize Yahweh remained unclear to first-century Jews. A variety of means by which the gentiles would come to recognize Yahweh as the

One God had been proposed. There was a small movement of missionary outreach, as evidenced in the book of Jonah, although its results were meager. In places, the apocalyptic literature speaks of a conquest of the nations and, at other places, of a miraculous coming of the gentiles to the light found in a renewed and purified Jerusalem (Zech. 8:23). Yet such questions were not critical for affirming Yahweh's sovereignty. Yahweh had revealed God's nature to the Hebrew people and called them to a particular form of obedience to the divine will. However, Jewish particularity did not mean that Yahweh is one god among many. Yahweh is Lord of all. The disclosure of God's universal sovereignty is to be at the end times. In the meantime, it is in Israel where a true knowledge of God is found and true worship given. In the interim, divine sovereignty over the nations does not require their conscious acknowledgement of divine will.

Early Christians modified the definition of particularism given in Judaism because they believed that Jesus is Lord of all now. In his resurrection-ascension, he received "the name which is above every name, that at the name of Jesus every knee should bow, in heaven and earth and under the earth" (Phil. 2:9–10). The response early Christians made to this Lordship was obedience to Jesus' command to make disciples of all people. Christ's Lordship over all is to be realized by calling people to faith in him. The success of this mission was such that by the fourth century Christianity had become the official religion of the Roman Empire and through it of Western civilization. Christianity had become "ecumenical." It had filled the *oikoumenē* and was coterminous with the whole inhabited earth as far as the world of the West was concerned (Matt. 24:14; Luke 2:1, 4:5; Rom. 10:18; et al.).

With the evangelizing of the northern European tribes, the British Isles, and the Balkans, the universality of the Lordship of Christ extended as far as the theologians and historians of the church of that time could see. The people of India, the Orient, sub-Sahara Africa, or the Americas were either unknown or existed only as marginal curiosities on the fringe of awareness. The universality or, as now it was called, the "catholicity" of the church had been fully realized. The anomaly is that in light of what really constitutes the whole world, this catholicity was rather limited and parochial in its scope.

Throughout the Middle Ages, reports of other civilizations and religions sparked an interest in missions like those of the Dominicans and Franciscans. In the fifteenth century, the philosopher Nicholas of Cusa (1401–64) envisaged a universal religion that would overcome the tragic differences that divided humankind and led to war. His vision, in *De Pace Fide*, witnessed to the legitimacy and value of the non-Christian religions.[1] Yet Western Christendom lived with little awareness of other religions, save for Judaism and Islam which were theologically encapsulated. The medieval Jew had been ghettoized by the Christians and turned into a nonperson whose religion was said to be a demonic caricature of the truth given to Christians alone. Islam was consigned to the status of infidel and enemy to be dealt with by force of arms. What truth was to be found in it was but a vestigial remain of the original revelation of God given to Noah.

The Lordship of Christ, Christians believed, until the early modern period, had been realized over the whole world through the agency of the church that bore his power of bestowing salvation or damnation through its means of grace. Christ was indeed Lord of all, even though men and women responded to that Lordship imperfectly. However, awareness of great areas of the world where the name of Jesus was unknown and other religions held sway played little part in medieval and Reformation theologies.[2] Even the attempts at forming a new theology of mission that would indigenize Christian faith to the culture of the non-Western world, like that of Matteo Ricci (1552–1610) and Raymond Lull (c.1233–c. 1315), were rejected. The universality of Christ had become tied to the spread of Western civilization and the church. The theological anomaly this posed for the Christian claim to universality stirred little concern.

The New Awareness

By the early sixteenth century, Europeans had entered an age of exploration and colonization that changed not only the social and political awareness of Western civilization but its religious consciousness as well. Slowly but undeniably, Western Christendom became aware of other religions and cultures untouched by faith in Christ. Christians became aware that their definition of the *oikoumenē*—"the whole inhabited earth"—was deficient. This new awareness of the world combined with the religious zeal sweeping Europe and America in the pietistic and revivalist movements of the seventeenth and eighteenth centuries to form a new commitment to mission. The universal Lordship of Christ over every place and people was to be realized through a missionary movement to make all peoples disciples of Christ. By the end of the eighteenth century, the modern missionary movement entered more than a century of expansion that brought Christianity into contact with all the major religions of the world. However, unlike the earlier missionary movement to the Roman Empire and the European tribes, the modern missionary movement did not witness the collapse of other religions and their replacement by Christianity. Herein lies the context that demands a fresh delineation of the Lordship of Christ.

The establishment of churches in non-Western lands has not been the prelude to the replacement of any but a few religious traditions. Buddhism, Hinduism, and Islam have responded to the challenge of Christianity by taking on new forms and renewed vitality in many places. Traditional tribal religions live on despite church growth. Today a reverse missionary movement is bringing non-Christian forms of spirituality to those for whom the culture religion of Western Christendom has broken down. The repulsing of Christianity by Marxism, both Leninist and Maoist, and by nationalistic religious movements has further constricted the scope of Christendom and limited the options for missionary work.

The contemporary religious situation gives no evidence that Christianity is to replace all other religions. Instead, there is growing awareness that religious pluralism will be permanent. This religious pluralism calls for a fresh enunciation of the Lordship of Christ. What does the Lordship of Christ mean in face of the continued existence and vitality of the non-Christian religions? How do we conceive Christ as Lord of all peoples when the opportunity for responding to him consciously is a live option for only a fraction of the world? The contemporary religious situation requires a new confession of God's disclosure to the whole world through Jesus Christ. However, the revelation in Jesus Christ cannot be confessed through religious fanaticism or through a secular indifference that equates all religions. We need to analyze what it means to confess the name of Jesus in a religiously plural world. We need to find a way to confess faith in the universality of God's Lordship shown in Christ that delivers us from both religious imperialism and religious indifference.

The Human Form of the Divine Name

The Christian proclamation of salvation through the "name of Jesus" implies more than knowing a personal name or being able to repeat theological formulas. To name the "name of Jesus" is to be put in touch with the divine power of salvation given in him. To know Christ's name is to know the mystery of his person. In the modern world, a name is a conventional label used to identify a person, place, or thing. Names do not, for us, have an essential relationship to what a person is or does. All our names have a meaning, at least when traced back to their origins, but our names are chosen, not for their ancient meaning, but as a matter of social convention or changing custom. Philosophically put, our ways of naming things are "nominalistic." A name is a tag conventionally selected and attached to a person to identify him or her. By contrast, in the ancient world and in many tribal societies today, the name of a person describes the being of that person. A name has ontological meaning; it tells what really is. Names express the inner reality of a person. When a person undergoes deeply significant change, he or she is given a new name.[3] To know the name of a person is to know what powers of being are at work in that person. To know the name "Jesus" and to call him "Lord" is to know the power of salvation. "Jesus the Lord" is the "name which is above every name" because it names the power of salvation. This name holds within itself all that Jesus is. His name sums up his life, death, and resurrection (Phil. 2:5–11).

According to primitive Christian preaching, Jesus was exalted to a new and higher status through his death and resurrection. "God has made him both Lord and Christ, this Jesus whom you crucified"

(Acts 2:36). Jesus, who had been prophet of the kingdom, healer, and teacher of righteousness (Acts 2:22), has been vindicated and exalted. This deliverance was not given to Jesus alone. Through him it is available to all humankind as a gift from God. Jesus, now known as Lord and Christ, is the Savior.

To confess the name of Jesus is to live by the pattern of salvation through death and rebirth revealed in him. The name of Jesus encodes the pattern of new being for all people. To invoke his name is to live by this new pattern of death and resurrection. Salvation comes to those who are willing to die to self and so be open to newness of life. Salvation is given when people cease trying to find meaning and security in what they make, shape, or control, and open themselves to the new life given in the Holy that transcends them. Human salvation is giving up the centers of meaning and security that are merely extensions of our own powers, to be resurrected into new being in dependence on God, whom we do not make, shape, or control.

The pattern of damnation is in grasping for security by our own means rather than being open to the future. To live in this way is, according to the New Testament, "living in the world" or "living by the flesh." Damnation is in the way of Adam, who sought equality with God. Salvation is the way of Jesus, who did not seek for equality with God, but took the way of self-emptying love. This way was vindicated by God in Jesus' resurrection-exaltation. Damnation was the fate of Lucifer, who said, "I will make myself like the Most High" (Isa. 14:14). Lucifer rejected the servant form. The Christ accepted it. To take the "form of a servant" and live in openness to the transcendent is the way of healing and renewal. To take the way of the servant by faith is to confess the name of Jesus by an act of commitment to the service of love to others. This dialectic of death and resurrection, through repentance and faith, may be analyzed by theological reflection. Theological formulas do not create this pattern of life; they reflect it. The priority is in the human act of faith in which people accept life in this pattern.

The problem before the early church was how to communicate this pattern of salvation in Jesus to those who live after the initial time of revelation. Two options for communicating the power of the name of Jesus were suggested to the early church from the religious milieu of its time: legalism and Gnosticism. (1) The saving power of the name could be communicated, as it had been among the Hebrews, by a legal code that gives precise meaning to the divine name in every particular human situation. (2) The saving name could be communicated as a secret word or magical formula given to the initiates, as in the Gnostic mystery religions.

Primitive Christianity rejected both of these alternatives. The Christian community affirmed that the saving name is not an esoteric magic formula, nor could it be defined by legal codes. The divine name had taken human form. "The Word became flesh and dwelt among us, full of grace and truth" (John 1:14). The name of Jesus is known by the form it takes in human existence. In Jesus, God is no longer remote but has entered the world of everyday life.

In postexilic Judaism, the holiness and transcendence of God has been emphasized to the point that the name of God was unmentionable for fear of blasphemy. The holiness of God had come to mean not simply transcendence but remoteness. The angelic hosts were the mediators who bore the divine commandments to humankind, and these commandments, now in the form of codified law, provided the basis for human beings to know and respond to God. The age of revelation had passed. What remained was a holy law that expressed the holiness of God. The holy name had been translated into a holiness code for the people of God.

In Gnosticism, God is also remote. The divine transcendence is defined in terms of God as the Abyss or Ground from which the heavenly hierarchy emerges but who is ultimately unmoved. The saving name is given by a savior lord to the believers so they can be reunited with the divine. The name is a secret word given to the initiate after careful preparation. The name cannot be "enfleshed," as was the divine Word in Jesus. Even the savior who brought the gnosis, the knowledge of God, was not really human but only appeared to be. For the Gnostic, divine reality is the antithesis of personal, human existence. The divine is known only through a disembodied secret word.

In rejecting legalism and Gnosticism, the church made clear its commitment to the human form the divine name had been given in

Jesus. The richness and complexity of human life cannot be reduced to a legal code or changed into esoteric knowledge entrusted to a few devotees. The divine name revealed in Jesus is revealed afresh wherever human life is being transformed.

Legalism and Gnosticism deny what is basic to Christianity, the conviction that God is personally present in a fully human life. Legalism and Gnosticism speak of an absent God who has sent information about himself. The revelation in Jesus embraces every level of human life. The revelation came in the Incarnate One and so continues to be incarnated. Response to revelation in Jesus is not merely a change of ideas but a change of being. Hence, no single ethical code, institutional form, or intellectual formula can comprehend the fullness of revelation in Jesus. Rather, every attempt to give institutional form or intellectual formulation to this revelation must itself be brought under critical judgment. This is something the church quickly forgot. The church took over "the name of Jesus" and changed it into a series of so-called "infallible" theological doctrines and equated the saving power of Jesus with its own means of grace. The church confused the power of salvation with the ways in which it confesses and celebrates that salvation. With its doctrinal and institutional exclusivism, the church has erected legalisms and gnosticisms of its own. The church confuses its reception of salvation with the scope of that salvation. The scope of salvation is universal while the witness to it given by the church is that of a particular religious community.

The Christian believes that the witness of Bible and church to revelation in Jesus is true. The biblical witness to revelation has priority for the Christian community in its thinking about all that God is doing in the world. The Presbyterian Church declares this in its *Confession of 1967* when it affirms the inspiration of the Bible as Word of God:

> The Scriptures are not a witness among others, but the witness without parallel. The church has received the books of the Old and New Testaments as prophetic and apostolic testimony in which it hears the word of God and by which its faith and obedience are nourished and regulated (1.C.2).

The Bible, interpreted in the power of the Spirit by the church, witnesses to revelation and, hence, is the means for discerning God's presence and activity in the world. However, the Christian is not committed to the belief that the church, or some part of it, is the only people of God. Nor is the Christian committed to the belief that the church has always been faithful to revelation. However, the Christian is committed to the belief that the disclosure of God in Jesus is authentic and that the biblical witness is decisive for its life. Hence, the Christian does not look first to the *Qur'an*, the *Rig-Veda*, the *Adi Granth*, the *Lotus Sutra*, or other religious writings when seeking guidance about God's self-disclosure. The Christian community looks first to the witness of its own Scriptures, confessions, and liturgies when making judgments about the presence and activity of God. From this primary witness, the Christian is able to look at other religious communities and discern when and where the saving power of God is at work in them.

The perception by Christians of God's presence in other religious communities and their Scriptures is derivative in character. The Christian moves outward from the revelation of God in Jesus as witnessed by Christian Scriptures and represented in its own sacraments and liturgies. The Christian perceptions of other religions are inevitably oblique and partial. The Christian approach to the sacred writings, ethical codes, and cultic actions of other traditions is from the basis of what is known of God through Jesus in the community of faith that has responded to him. By contrast, the Muslim looks directly at the *Qur'an* as the Word of God. The Christian looks at the *Qur'an* and is able to see in it evidences of the Word of God.[4] The Hindu looks directly to the *Upanishads* as the divinely given message of liberation. The Christian may see in the *Upanishads* a witness to new being through a death to the self, and in seeing this, the Christian may affirm it as God's gift of new being through death and resurrection.[5] By sharing in the liturgical and communal life of the church, the Christian is enabled to discern the redemptive presence of God in the liturgies, communal meals, and ethical codes of other communities of faith.

The perception of God's redemptive presence in other religious traditions and communities is not the uncritical acceptance of everything called religious. Human religiousness, just as every other human activity, is subject to sin. By the light given in Jesus, however,

the Christian community is able to perceive the light of God found
in other places. The revelation in Jesus is not only intelligible itself;
it makes other things intelligible also.[6] The light of the gospel allows
Christians to make negative as well as positive discernments about
other religious traditions. Negatively, the gospel exposes human sin-
fulness. "And this is the judgment, that the light has come into the
world, and men loved darkness rather than light, because their deeds
were evil" (John 3:19). Positively, the gospel makes evident
truth wherever it is found: "when anything is exposed by the
light it becomes visible, for anything that becomes visible is light"
(Eph. 5:13).

Beyond the Tribal God

When early Christians tried to relate the understanding
of the universality of Yahweh learned from their Jewish background,
they encountered severe theological problems. Most of the common-
sense answers people gave about how God was present in this person
Jesus seemed always to end in heresy. What was required was a
complete recasting of the ways in which people think about God.
While holding onto its conviction of the unity of God, the church
found a way of confessing the authenticity of divine presence in
Jesus and the Holy Spirit through the doctrine of the Trinity. The
doctrine of the Trinity links the universal sovereignty of God the
Creator to the particular personal appearance of God in Jesus and in
the heart of the believer through the Spirit. The doctrine of the
Trinity affirms that at no point does God deal with us at second
hand. The one God is confessed as a Trinity—Creator, Redeemer,
and Perfecter—in such a way that there is one God, not three. Each
person of the Trinity has particular functions of its own, yet the
persons coinhere. When God acts to create and sustain as Father,
reveal and redeem as Son, or sanctify and fulfill as Spirit, it is an
action of the whole Trinity. Conversely, what can be said of the
whole Trinity can be said of each member of the Trinity. The omnipresence of the triune God means that the Creator, Redeemer, and
Sanctifier are present in all places and all times.

The church confesses that Jesus Christ is the Second Person of the Trinity incarnate. While Jesus' earthly ministry took place in a particular place and time, his continuing work as Second Person of the Trinity is universal in scope. In resurrection and ascension, Jesus is exalted to share fully in the divine life. Jesus, as exalted Lord, is omnipresent. The logic of trinitarianism is clear on this point. However, Christians have had great difficulty in accepting its implications. The doctrine of the Trinity repudiates the persistent human attempt to make God into a regional God dependent on particular people and their religious ideas. God is who God is in revelation. What was revealed of God in Jesus is what God is like in all places, not just in those places where God is confessed as the Trinity or named by the church.

Theologians of the neo-orthodox and biblical theology schools have tried to protect the uniqueness of Christian doctrine of God by speaking of "the God of the Bible," "the God of the Christian faith," or even "the God of Jesus." These theologians wanted to be sure that what they were saying about God would not be confused with what others were saying about God. So they opposed "the God of the Bible" to "the God of the Hindus," "the God of the Muslims," or any other conception of God. Unfortunately, this apologetic move undermines what is most central to the biblical witness to the reality of God. There is only one God. Although conceived of in many different ways, God remains one. God is present and active in the whole created order, not just in the places where confessed and worshipped by the church. No religious forms or theological teachings give God universality. God has this characteristic already. Hence, the questions to be asked when encountering other religious communities need to be changed. The problem of the missionary is not how we can bring God to some place. God is there already. We need instead to look at what it means to say that God is present in the whole world, including its religious traditions, communities, and life. It is at this point that the doctrine of the Trinity can be of help.

The Second Person of the Trinity is God's agent in creating and sustaining the world. The Second Person of the Trinity is the Logos which gives to all reality its logical and ethical structure and meaning. The Second Person of the Trinity is the agent of the divine providence who keeps the world from falling into chaos. Thus in

God's creating, sustaining, and redeeming the world, the Second Person of the Trinity is present in the whole world. There are no godless places in the world, even though people, at times, act as if there were.

Jesus of Nazareth is the Second Person of the Trinity incarnate. Hence, by knowing Jesus through his life, death, and resurrection, it is possible to know God because God is what God is revealed to be. Jesus is not simply a prophetic teacher who brings new information about God. Jesus is the act of God in which God is personally present. Jesus gives human expression to what God is doing in the whole world for human salvation. He embodies God's gift of new being through death and resurrection. Wherever God is present as Second Person of the Trinity, there the power of salvation revealed in Jesus is also present. In light of the doctrine of the Trinity, it is impossible to speak of "bringing Christ" to any part of the world. As risen and exalted Lord, Christ is present and awaits us already.[7] The proclamation of the gospel allows people to respond to that presence, but it does not create that presence.

Since God is not regional but omnipresent, what does the doctrine of the Trinity imply about the non-Christian religious traditions? Negatively, there are not many gods and many sources of good. God is one and is the ultimate source of all the good in the world. The saving act of God in Christ is the one all-sufficient source of salvation. What is plural are the responses people make to God's saving presence in the world.

Positively, in gracious freedom God utilizes not only Christianity but also the worship, institutions, and traditions of other religious communities to bring salvation to humankind. Judgments are made about God's redemptive presence in the world, for those who live within the Christian community, in light of the pattern of salvation revealed by Jesus. The life, death, and resurrection of Jesus are not simply historical events isolated in first-century Palestine. They are the pattern of new being. What is revealed in that particular place is universal in scope. They disclose an ontological structure through which human existence is transformed. This structure of new being is not merely a psychological insight given by Jesus, the religious teacher, although it has obvious psychological meaning. Instead, wherever the dialectic of death and renewal, of alienation and reconciliation, of repentance and faith is present, the power of the Second Person of the Trinity is present. Because of its basis in God, this pattern of salvation is universal in its scope.

Hence, whenever religious tradition turns people from their present finite centers of security and meaning to finding new being in the transcendent, that tradition becomes a means of salvation.

Wherever a religious community, through its worship, teaching, and life, moves people away from giving ultimate allegiance to things they make, shape, or control toward finding life in the Holy, that religion becomes a means of grace.

As a religious tradition allows people to be open to others and to the world, that tradition is a means of healing and renewal.

Whenever a religion enables people to live in such a way as to believe that the future will meet them as love, that religion is a means of salvation.

Whenever a religion frees a person from trusting in his or her own power, goodness, and strength, and points a believer toward finding salvation in the Holy, that religion is a channel of new being.

When a religious community makes its own cultus, doctrine, or institutions the source of salvation instead of the transcendent power of the Holy, that community is *not* a means of grace.

To the measure that a religion encourages people to give their highest loyalty to a given political, racial, ideological, or economic order, that religion is a source of damnation.

Wherever the religious life is motivated by hatred, fear, and a sense of superiority over others, it is a way of life that leads to destruction.

The One and the Many

It is important at this point to sort out, from the Christian perspective, what is plural and what unitary in human salvation. God, confessed by Christians as Creator, Redeemer, and Perfecter, is the one source of goodness. God is encountered by religious communities as the Holy and Transcendent to which they seek to respond by their faith and express in their worship, teachings, and communal life. The response of the various religious communities is plural. It takes many forms. Some of these religious responses to the Holy are creative and healing. Other responses are distorted and self-serving.

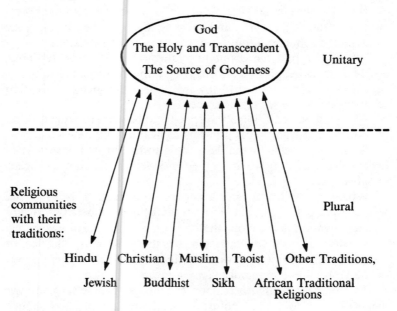

These communities of faith are linked to the Holy by a two-way process. Believers in these communities respond to the disclosures of the Holy. The revelation of the Holy shapes and directs these communities although this response is never perfect.

This diagram presents Christianity in one of its aspects. It is a religion among religions with its own unique, historically given forms and ways. As a religion it has similarities to many other religions. As a religion, it is both a response to the revelation of God and the human denial of that revelation. The Christian religion is under both the blessing of God and the judgment of God. Christianity has witnessed to God against the idolatrous powers of this world, and it has also been involved in supporting these powers.

Another viewpoint is needed to give the full picture of how Christians understand their relationship to God. The Christian community is a bearer of the unique witness to the revelation of God in Jesus Christ. Through its Scriptures and confessions, the church witnesses to the revelation that is normative for its understanding of God's presence in the world. While the church is able to affirm God's redemptive presence in the whole world, it makes this affirmation on the basis of what it has first known of God through Jesus Christ. Its Scripture has the priority for shaping the faith of the Christian. By what the church knows of God, revealed by the Spirit through Christ, it is able to orient itself in relation to other religious communities. This orientation allows the Christian faith community to affirm the goodness and renewal that is God's gift wherever it is found. It also allows this faith community to see the perversions and distortions that are part of all religious traditions, including its own.

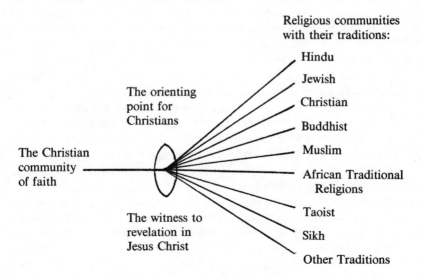

This diagram illustrates those aspects of Christian tradition that calls the church elect. When the church is referred to as "the elect," it is being described in light of God's election of this people to be the bearers of divine revelation in Jesus. To call the church "elect" does not mean its members alone are saved. It is elect by virtue of being the servant people who bear witness to the revelation in Jesus, but the mystery of this election is that it is not dependent on the supposedly superior virtue of the church. It is dependent on the sovereign grace of God. When the church forgets this and tries to make itself the supreme and only locus of faithfulness to God, it forfeits its work as witness to the universal love of God.

Heresy and Orthodoxy

The question of orthodoxy and heresy comes into new perspective when considered in a religiously plural world. The test of orthodoxy has been in the establishment of continuity in language between biblical and earlier orthodox confessional statements and a new theological formulation. The determination of orthodoxy was formal and logical and based on the establishment of identity in verbal forms. Emphasis was on the change of one verbal form into another. This method works as long as the changes in verbal forms occur within the same cultural group, but when the basic presuppositions of life undergo radical change, the mere transposition of verbal forms into those of another language is not sufficient.

The problems of Christological heresy would not have been as difficult for the early church as they were if the only problem was that of changing Hebrew and Aramaic terms into Latin and Greek. Every language has its implicit religious vision and worldview. Problems of similar complexity face the church today in its search for faithfulness. Establishing norms for orthodoxy today cannot be settled by reference to ancient or Reformation creeds and confessions. As useful as these confessions have been, their work of witness was made in cultural patterns that are remote from the situation in which questions of right belief are being asked today. Historical understanding may illuminate differences in understanding from past ages, but it does not overcome them. Alienation from the premodern thought patterns has forced upon theology in Europe and America the need for finding new techniques for determining orthodoxy. However, the problems are most acute as theology moves from the European-American context to those of Africa, Asia, and Latin America. Here the cultural differences are immense and hold little promise of being bridged.

Orthodox translations of the name of Jesus express his universality. Orthodox Christology points to the reality of salvation in Christ and allows participation in it. Christological language is not the saving reality, but it is a way in which humans share in that reality. Faith is faith in Jesus, not faith in the truth of certain information about him. So the test of orthodoxy is functional.[8] The orthodoxy of any expression of the meaning of Jesus is the measure to which it facilitates the life of death and resurrection. This is possible because the grounds for the translatability of the name of Jesus are not merely verbal but ontological. As risen Lord, Jesus is the source of that saving power the world itself cannot produce. The ability to "name" the source of salvation is not based on transmitting an esoteric word or law code of holiness. It is based on the presence of Christ in which people participate. They learn to give up the old self and to be reborn into a new self. Heretical translations of the saving name are those that block or pervert participation in his being. Heresy is any ideology that allows people to live from their own idolatrous means of security. Heresy sanctifies what we make, shape, and control as the source of meaning.

The Way of the Church

With the triumph of Christianity as the religion of the West, the means of participating in Christ's salvation were limited to the preaching and sacraments of the church. As Cyprian expressed it, "Outside the church, no salvation." The effect of this emphasis on the means of grace found in the church alone was to change the character of the church. The church was no longer seen as a witnessing people who point to a source of salvation that transcends the church and is capable of judging it. Instead, the church marked the limits of salvation. It became the ark of salvation in a sea of damnation. The universality of Christ became equated with the universality of the church, but this is a misunderstanding of the universality of Jesus. It is more accurate to say that the church points to the power of salvation found in it, but this power extends beyond it into the whole world. This universality belongs to Jesus Christ.

In the church, Jesus is known by his name and is shared by preaching and sacraments that actualize his presence. His presence as confessed there, through the witness of Scripture and Spirit, is normative for discerning his presence and work in the world. But the preaching and sacraments of the church are not the only means of grace. The power of the saving name reaches beyond the traditions of the church. The traditions of other religions are used by God for people to share in the new being. Wherever human existence is marked by a self-abandoning trust that is ready to give up present centers of security in openness to the transcendent, such life is evidence of the presence of the kingdom.

The church is, in this regard, analogous to ancient Israel. The sovereignty of God to which the Hebrews responded through revelation is a sovereignty that moves all the nations, whether they acknowledge it or not. The function of the church, like the function of Israel, is to act as a community of witness. This witness by words and deeds points to the universal sovereignty and redemptive love of God in Christ. The church makes this witness most fully when it is most deeply faithful to Christ. What is envisaged is not religious syncretism but a Christian witness that does not confuse the particularity of its own formulations with the scope of God's activity. Wherever life is broken free of sin and death, this freedom comes from Jesus Christ, even though it may be apprehended in forms that are not specifically Christian.

Christian theology has differed in the ways in which it identifies the sources of human goodness and fulfillment for those who are outside the church. One tradition has held that the only real virtue is that which comes from a conscious relationship to Christ and the church. Others have argued for the existence of genuine goodness apart from conscious recognition of Jesus or the teachings of the church. Christian triumphalism followed Augustine who maintained that the virtues of the pagans are but "splendid vices." The best Augustine could say of non-Christian life was that while pagans were pursuing certain vices, such as pride and vain national glory, other vices, such as civil disorder and debauchery, were restrained.[9] To follow this logic is to fall into the error of calling goodness evil. Faithfulness to Jesus does not require the denigration of human goodness except as it is found in the church. Wherever human life is being renewed, there the kingdom of God is present because God alone is the source of goodness although there are many ways in which it is expressed to the world.

As Wilfred C. Smith (b. 1916) argues, the question of how the religious traditions of the world function in human salvation is, at least on the mundane level, a historical question. We know that through them people have been

> saved from nihilism, from alienation, anomie, despair; from the bleak despondency of meaninglessness. Saved from unfreedom; saved from being the victims of one's own whims within, or of pressures without; saved from being merely an organism reacting to its environment.[10]

No matter how infrequently they may be found in this sinful world, love, forgiveness, courage, and hope are found in religious communities. Christians do not have a monopoly on them. While we may treasure the revelation of salvation given in the history of the Christian religious community, it is impossible to deny the work of God in other religious communities. While we confess that the *Heilsgeschichte* of ancient Israel and the church is crucial for our faith, we cannot deny the work of God in other traditions. In this sense, Smith is right in observing: "All human history is *Heilsgeschichte*."[11]

In the gift of salvation, God expresses divine freedom to be "for us" by creating opportunities for human renewal throughout creation. Where human life is being debased, there the power of new being is being rejected, no matter what religious traditions, including those of Christianity, are being invoked. The Christological norm is the principle of judgment against Christianity as well as against other religions.

Missions and Universalism

Recognition of the freedom of God to provide means for salvation when, where, and how God wills does not negate the evangelistic mission of the church. The freedom of universality is God's freedom and not ours. The church is to maintain its character as the community commissioned to witness to Jesus Christ through its words and actions. Knowing the source of new being in Jesus' name, the church proclaims him and the kingdom to all the world. In doing this, the church is not bringing Jesus and the kingdom to a world to which Christ is a stranger. The proclamation of the church about Jesus is a way in which people respond to the kingdom by faith and obedience. The evangelizing mission of the church is responsive to the presence of the kingdom but does not control it. The church is not given the power to dictate what form response to the proclamation about Jesus shall take. The primary response Christian missions seek is the baptism and reception into the church of those who have lived by other religious traditions, but there are other responses which God uses in human salvation. The preaching of the gospel in many parts of the world has resulted in few converts. Yet the power of the gospel to illumine the destructive and dehumanizing aspects of human religiousness has led to fundamental changes in other religious traditions even when they were not abandoned for Christianity.[12]

In its witness to the kingdom, the church is not called on to be successful but to be faithful. The proclamation of the gospel is done in the confidence that words and deeds empowered by the Spirit become God's word and, therefore, will not fail to fulfill his purposes, even when we cannot identify this fulfillment (Isa. 55:10–11). Where the number of people who enter the Christian community as baptized believers is small, missions cannot be said to have failed; nor where there is church growth of astounding proportions can the mission be said to have succeeded. In every case, there remains a mystery about how God calls peoples to himself. Whether the response to proclamation is the growth of churches or the restructuring and renewal of other religious communities is not at the disposal of those who make the witness. The church proclaims a human liberation in Jesus Christ that goes beyond the limits of its institutions to transform social, political, economic, and intellectual life in ways unexpected by those who bear witness. The crucial matter is that the Christian witness is faithful to Jesus in proclaiming God's renewal of the world on all levels of being.

The universality of new being in Christ raises the question of universalism in salvation. The term "universalism" has been used in two ways. Universalism can indicate the universal availability of salvation of all humankind, or it can indicate that all persons are saved. This first definition of universalism is grounded in the gospel itself. The invitation is to whosoever believes and is given without partiality to race or nation (John 3:16). However, to declare the universal possibility of salvation does not imply the universal actuality of salvation. The second definition of universalism is an unwarranted speculation about the judgments of God. It is clear from Scripture that the being of God is both one of judgment and mercy. What is not given to us is how this dialectic is resolved for every person or group.

Affirming the universal availability of salvation is a protest against the demonic particularism of those who are positive they know who will or will not be saved. In the face of the mystery of salvation, the church is called to witness to the power of salvation but not to determine how people have responded to this witness. Pronouncements about either damnation or universal salvation remain speculative because God alone is judge of human hearts. Before the mystery of God's call and human response, the only legitimate response is doxological. Paul, as he contemplated the mystery of alienation and reconciliation of his own people, Israel, made the only requisite conclusion, "O the depth of the riches and wisdom and knowledge of God! How unsearchable are his judgments and how inscrutable his ways!" (Rom. 11:33).

The Center and the Fence

Christians give centrality in their faith to Jesus Christ. The problem is how to maintain this centrality. The church has maintained it by making itself a boundary community. It has protected the absoluteness of Jesus Christ by erecting a fence around itself, marking it off from other groups. This fence has taken the form of doctrinal formularies, ethical codes, liturgical forms, or adherence to a particular form of church organization. This act of fencing was to affirm and protect what is central to Christian faith—

the person and work of Jesus. By clearly defining what is Christian and what is not, it is possible to maintain orthodoxy and, hence, a saving relationship to Jesus Christ. The difficulty in fencing off Christendom from all the rest of the world is what it did to Christians. It brought about a terrifying arrogance that led Christians to justify their use of social, psychological, political, economic, and military power to enforce their will on others. It sectionalized the world into areas of light and darkness, truth and error, by separating them with religious fences. Such an act denies the freedom of God. It leads to the demonism of believing that Christians have to make the world safe for Christ and the kingdom by defeating all of Christ's enemies who are naturally also their enemies. The ghastly history of Christian involvement in inquisitions, Crusades, and the Holocaust shows the frightening cost of such a theology.

The fence mentality takes the emphasis away from Jesus and places it on the theological and institutional structures that have been reared in God's name. This shift is from the affirmation of "apart from Christ, no salvation" to "Outside the church, no salvation." Such a shift is not legitimate. The fence mentality has not protected the redemptive power of Christ but has shifted it to the institutions of Christendom. In place of the fence mentality, there is a need to reaffirm the centrality of Jesus Christ. When it is possible to express adequately the meaning of Jesus Christ, fences will become irrelevant.

Christian faith is best expressed not by drawing a fence but by defining a center. By defining the center of new life given in Jesus, it is possible to see how the divine redemptive power is at work in the world. To clarify the forms and presence of new being is to affirm and join with Jesus in moving the world closer to the full humanity given in him. By dropping the fence mentality, the Christian community will be freed of the defensiveness that has marred its witness to Christ's love. We do not need to protect Christ and the kingdom from enemies. Jesus Christ is Lord already. The powers of the kingdom are already more real than the powers of destructiveness in the world. The kingdom of God as revealed in Jesus may become actual at any point in the world because it is universal already. What Christian witness does is to provide awareness of its presence and meaning.

The task of theological reflection is not to create a new dogmatic legalism to protect Christ but to explicate the new humanity given in him. The creeds, confessions, and theologies of the church clarify the unique relationship of the human and divine in Jesus Christ. This divine-human relationship is the basis of Christ's redemptive work and explicates the presence of new being to a world where it is obscured by sin and death. The church is the community of witness to a salvation at work within and beyond itself. The confession of Jesus Christ provides the means for judging the perversions in all religious traditions, including our own. It is the means for finding where new life is at work in other traditions, so that Jesus Christ may be affirmed and joined in leading people to fuller participation in the kingdom.

Notes

PART I: REASONS FOR HOPE

1. Franz Rosenzweig, *Briefe und Tagebücher*, ed. Edith Rosenzweig (Berlin: Shocken Verlag, 1935), 690 (author's trans.).

CHAPTER 1: FAITH AND THOUGHT

1. Edward Rochie Hardy, ed., *Christology of the Later Fathers* (Philadelphia: Westminster Press, 1954), 18.
2. The use of personalistic categories for reinterpreting Christology became prominent in the work of P. T. Forsyth, *The Person and Place of Jesus Christ* (London: Congregational Union of England and Wales, 1909; reprint ed., Independent Press, 1955), in which he sets forth his new methodology for "The Moralizing of Dogma," 213–57. Personal categories are basic for the mediating Christology of Donald Baillie, *God Was in Christ* (New York: Charles Scribner's Sons, 1948), 106–79 However, behind this personalistic tradition in the English-speaking world is the work of the German mediating theologians of the nineteenth century. Isaak Dorner, for example, in his *Entwicklungsgeschichte der Lehre von der Person Christi* (Stuttgart: 1839, 2d ed. 4 vols., 1846–56), saw in modern times a new philosophy and poetry emerging that delivered Christology from dependence on the abstract impersonal categories of ancient metaphysics. For an analysis of this background, see my book *The Form of a Servant* (Philadelphia: Westminster Press, 1963), 86–126.
3. For an analysis of the existentialist, process, and linguistic analytic Christologies, see my article "Christology in Contemporary Systematic Theology," *Interpretation* 26 (1972): 259–77. Since that time, the process approach to Christology has been enlarged by David Ray Griffin, *A Process Christology* (Philadelphia: Westminster Press, 1973), and Lewis S. Ford, *The Lure of God: A Biblical Background to Process Theism* (Philadelphia: Fortress Press, 1978), 45–70. One of the most provocative developments of Christologies related to linguistic analytic thought is that of David Tracy, *Blessed Rage for Order* (New York: Seabury Press, 1975), 204–36.
4. William Hamilton and Thomas J. J. Altizer, *Radical Theology and the Death of God* (Indianapolis: Bobbs-Merrill Co., 1966) is the fundamental statement of the "death of God" Christologies. For an analysis of this literature, see John A. Phillips, "Radical Christology: Jesus and the Death of God," *Cross Currents* 19 (1969): 273–96. The basis for a humanistic Marxist interpretation of Jesus is given by Ernst Bloch, *Das*

Prinzip Hoffnung, 2 vols. (Frankfurt: Suhrkamp Verlag, 1959), 2: 1412 ff. An example of the use of the depth psychology of Carl G. Jung as the basis of a Christology is found in Edward F. Edinger, *Ego and Archetype* (New York: G. P. Putnam's Sons, 1972), 131–56. A fascinating but unproductive attempt to build a modernist Christology based on depth psychology is that of G. Stanley Hall, *Jesus, the Christ, in the Light of Psychology* (New York: Doubleday, Page, & Co., 1917).

5. Rubem A. Alves initiated the development of a Christology in the Latin American tradition of liberation theology with his treatment of the dual themes of messianic humanism and humanistic messianism in *A Theology of Human Hope* (Washington: Corpus Books, 1969). Since then, there has been a tremendous proliferation of literature in this area. The fullest contemporary statement of a liberation Christology is that of Jon Sobrino, S.J., *Christology at the Crossroads,* trans. John Drury (Maryknoll: Orbis Books, 1978).

The folk religion of Black America was given visibility as the basis of a Christology of liberation in Albert B. Cleage, Jr., *The Black Messiah* (New York: Sheed and Ward, 1968). James H. Cone (b. 1938) links the Black understanding of Christ to current academic developments in theology, *A Black Theology of Liberation* (Philadelphia: J. B. Lippincott Co., 1970), 203–19.

Early leaders of the movement for the liberation of women found a champion for the rejection of the legal codes that enslaved them in Jesus. Elizabeth Cady Stanton and Lucy Stone used Jesus' reinterpretation of the biblical laws as the authorization for their reinterpreting biblical and church laws, but the feminist movement has increasingly turned away from a male Jesus as an adequate symbol of their struggle. See Naomi R. Goldenberg, *Changing of the Gods* (Boston: Beacon Press, 1979), 1–9, and Mary Daly, *Beyond God the Father* (Boston: Beacon Press, 1973), 69–97.

A helpful study of the development of a Christology free of anti-Semitism and the extensive literature related to it is given by Michael B. McGarry, C.S.P., *Christology after Auschwitz* (New York: Paulist Press, 1977). A more pessimistic appraisal of the present status of the development of a Christology free of anti-Semitism is that of Robert E. Willis, "Christian Theology after Auschwitz," *Journal of Ecumenical Studies* 12 (1975): 493–519.

6. For an introduction to the emerging Christologies related to non-Christian religious traditions, see my article, "Christology in Contemporary Systematic Theology" and Lucien Richard, O.M.I., "Some Recent Developments on the Question of Christology and the Third World," *Église et Théologie* 8 (1977): 209–44.

7. The most comprehensive model for this approach to Christology is Isaak A. Dorner, *Entwicklungsgeschichte der Lehre von der Person*

Christi, which subsequently appeared in a five-volume English translation, *History of the Development of the Doctrine of the Person of Christ*
(Edinburgh: T. & T. Clark, 1891). He sought to establish patterns of
historical development that were to serve as trajectories to guide further
developments.
8. Ernst Troeltsch, *Der Historismus und seine Probleme* found in *Gesammelte Schriften* (Tübingen: Verlag von J. C. B. Mohr, 1922), 3:656.
9. Austin Farrer, "An English Appreciation," in Hans Werner Bartsch,
ed., *Kerygma and Myth*, trans. Reginald H. Fuller (London: S.P.C.K.,
1957), 213.
10. Michel Foucault, *The Birth of the Clinic*, trans. A. M. Sheridan Smith
(New York: Vintage Books, 1975), xix.
11. A Christology within the classical tradition written in the modern times
is that of the Roman Catholic theologian, Karl Adam, *The Christ of
Faith*, trans. Joyce Crick (New York: New American Library, Mentor
Omega Books, 1962). Eric Mascall, Paul Althaus, and from a very different perspective, Carl Henry have worked within the classical tradition to
build a modern Christology. The desideratum of such Christologies is
that they look upon the hypostatic union of the two natures as the basis
for what they say about the historical Jesus instead of viewing incarnation as a conclusion to be reached by reflection on the Christ event as a
whole.
12. John H. Leith, ed., *Creeds of the Churches*, 3d ed. (Atlanta: John Knox
Press, 1982), 36.
13. Gotthold Ephraim Lessing, "Ueber den Beweis des Geistes und der
Kraft," *Gesammelte Werke*, ed. Paul Rilla (Berlin: Aufbau Verlag,
1956), 8: 9–10.
14. Immanuel Kant, *Critique of Practical Reason*, trans. T. K. Abbott
(London: Longmans, Green and Co., 1948), 229.
15. For an analysis of the conception of the *Vorstellung* in Hegel, see Dawe,
The Form of a Servant, 104–26.
16. Friedrich Schleiermacher, *The Christian Faith*, ed. H. R. Mackintosh
and J. S. Stewart (Edinburgh: T. & T. Clark, 1928), 94: 385.
17. Neill Hamilton, *Jesus for a No-God World* (Philadelphia: Westminster
Press, 1969).
18. A Christology of this type was formulated by Dorothee Sölle by reversing the traditional doctrine of Christ as the representative of humankind. It is, for her, not that in Jesus Christ, God steps into the place of
humanity to reveal the divine essence and bear human sin. Since God
does not yet exist, Jesus Christ steps into the place of the absent God on
behalf of humankind. See her *Christ the Representative*, trans. David
Lewis (Philadelphia: Fortress Press, 1967), 132.
19. Søren Kierkegaard, *Philosophical Fragments*, trans. David F. Swenson
(Princeton: Princeton University Press, 1936), 29–38.

20. Daniel Bell, "The Return of the Sacred?" *British Journal of Sociology* 28 (1972): 429.
21. Kierkegaard, *Philosophical Fragments*, 5–16.
22. Adam, *The Christ of Faith*, 266.
23. Lars Thunberg, *Microcosm and Mediator* (Lund: C. W. K. Gleerup, 1965), 21–37.
24. For the history of this term, see August Deneffe, S.J., "Perichoresis, Circumincessio, Circuminsessio," *Zeitschrift fur katholische Theologie* 47 (1923): 497–532.
25. For an analysis of the logic of coinherence see Thunberg, 28–37; Harry Austryn Wolfson, *The Philosophy of the Church Fathers*, 2d ed. (Cambridge, Mass.: Harvard University Press, 1964), 1: 418–28; J. F. Bethune-Baker, *An Introduction to the Early History of Christian Doctrine* (London: Methun & Co., Ltd., 1903), 226, 293–94; J. N. D. Kelly, *Early Christian Doctrines*, 2d ed. (London: Adam & Charles Black, 1960), 280–301; Aloys Grillmeier, "Die theologische und sprachliche Vorbereitung der christologischen Formel von Chalkedon," and Charles Moeller, "Le chalcedonisme et le neo-chalcedonisme," *Das Konzil von Chalkedon* (Wuerzburg: Echter Verlag, 1951), 1: 160–202 and 704–20. For a contrasting view see George Leonard Prestige, *"Perichoreo* and *Perichoresis* in the Fathers," *The Journal of Theological Studies* 29 (1928): 242–52 and his *God in Patristic Thought* (London: S.P.C.K., 1952), 282–301.
26. Wolfhart Pannenberg, "The Crisis of the Scripture Principle," *Basic Questions in Theology*, 2 vols., trans. George H. Kehm (Philadelphia: Fortress Press, 1970–71), 1: 1–14. Brevard S. Childs, *Biblical Theology in Crisis* (Philadelphia: Westminster Press, 1970), 51–87.
27. Brevard S. Childs, *Introduction to the Old Testament as Scripture* (Philadelphia: Fortress Press, 1979), 46–83, deals with canon as the context for interpreting the Old Testament.
28. Leith, *Creeds of the Churches*, 196.
29. Paul Ricoeur, "Biblical Hermeneutics," *Semeia 4*, ed. John Dominic Crossan (Missoula, Mont.: Scholars Press, 1975), 29–148 and *Interpretation Theory* (Fort Worth: Texas Christian University Press, 1976), 1–44 and 71–95. Tracy, *Blessed Rage for Order*, 119–145. A related development may be seen in Anton Grabner-Haider, ed., *Die Bibel und unsere Sprache: Konkrete Hermeneutik* (Wien: Herder, 1970), the Christological articles, 87 ff.

CHAPTER 2: THE MAN JESUS
AND THE COMING CHRIST

1. For the history of this development see Donald G. Dawe, *No Orthodoxy but the Truth* (Philadelphia: Westminster Press, 1969), 11–55 and 151–68.

2. While his conclusions are unconvincing, Malachi Martin has written an interesting history of the changing religious and cultural pictures of Jesus including those found in contemporary pop culture, *Jesus Now* (New York: E. P. Dutton & Co., Inc., 1973), 5–110.
3. The literature of this movement is immense. A start on it in English translation is Claude Welch, ed., *God and Incarnation in Mid-Nineteenth Century German Theology* (New York: Oxford University Press, 1965). There is an analysis of the mediating Christologies in Dawe, *The Form of a Servant*, 86–155. For a detailed treatment of Dorner see Charles L. Hargis, "The Concept of the Incarnation of God in the Thought of Isaak Dorner" (Ph.D. diss. Union Theological Seminary in Virginia, 1974).
4. Albert Schweitzer, *The Quest of the Historical Jesus*, trans. W. Montgomery (New York: The Macmillan Co., 1955), 398–403. Later Schweitzer spoke of his going to the mission hospital in Lambarene as such an act of discipleship. He said, "I am in Africa by a command of Jesus."
5. Augustine, *The City of God*, trans. Marcus Dods, 2 vols. (New York: Hafner Publishing Co., 1948), 12.17; 20.5; Mircea Eliade, *Cosmos and History*, trans. Willard R. Trask (New York: Harper Torchbooks, 1959), 112–62.
6. Martin Werner, *The Formation of Christian Dogma*, trans. S. G. F. Brandon (New York: Harper & Brothers, 1957), 43.
7. Konrad Lorenz, *On Aggression*, trans. Marjorie K. Wilson (New York: Harcourt, Brace & World, 1966). An attempt has been made to extend the results of ethological research to specific moral and religious questions as in Wolfgang Wickler, *The Biology of the Ten Commandments*, trans. David Smith (New York: McGraw-Hill Book Co., 1972). Wickler makes the same reductionistic explanations of human behavior as does Lorenz although his conclusions are somewhat more optimistic. His approach to the history of religions is far from convincing. The new mythology of the all-determining gene is given classic expression in Richard Dawkins, *The Selfish Gene* (Oxford: Oxford University Press, 1976).

   An attempt to deal with this kind of thinking is found in Lawrence G. Miller, "Fated Gene," *The Sociobiology Debate*, ed. Arthur L. Caplan (New York: Harper & Row, 1979), 269–79. A methodological critique of Edward Wilson's attempt to build a comprehensive model of human life and culture on a genetic basis is given by Richard M. Burrian, "A Methodological Critique of Sociobiology," Caplan, 376–95. The attempt to answer critics and reformulate is in Charles J. Lumsden and Edward O. Wilson, *Promethean Fire* (Cambridge, Mass.: Harvard University Press, 1984).
8. Robert C. Tucker, *Philosophy and Myth in Karl Marx* (Cambridge: Cambridge University Press, 1965), 123–61. Gustav A. Wetter, *Dialecti-*

cal Materialism, trans. Peter Heath (New York: Frederick A. Praeger, 1959), 310–65.

9. Wolfhart Pannenberg, *What Is Man? Contemporary Anthropology in Theological Perspective*, trans. Duane A. Priebe (Philadelphia: Fortress Press, 1970), 1–27.

10. Alan Richardson, "Salvation," *The Interpreter's Dictionary of the Bible*, ed. George Arthur Buttrick (New York: Abingdon Press, 1962), 4: 168–81. The analysis of the basic metaphors that characterize the understanding of salvation in other religious traditions will be developed more fully later in this book. For a typological analysis of conceptions of salvation see my article "Salvation," *Abingdon Dictionary of Living Religions*, ed. Keith Crim (Nashville: Abingdon Press, 1981), 643–46.

11. Ernst Troeltsch, "Historiography," *Encyclopaedia of Religion and Ethics*, ed. James Hastings (New York: Charles Scribner's Sons, 1914), 6: 716–23. R. G. Collingwood, *The Idea of History* (New York: Oxford University Press, 1946), 231–315. The specification of modern historiography for research in the Gospels is given by Norman Perrin, *Rediscovering the Teachings of Jesus* (London: S.C.M. Press, 1957), 15–53.

12. Troeltsch, "Ueber historische und dogmatische Methode in der Theologie," *Gesammelte Schriften* (Tübingen: Verlag von J. C. B. Mohr, 1913; Aalen, Scientia Verlag, 1951-77), 2:729–53, and his "Historiography," *Encyclopaedia of Religion and Ethics*, 6: 718–19.

13. A recent attempt was made to reissue the old rationalistic idea of the resurrection as return after an apparent death stage managed by Jesus. See Hugh J. Schonfield, *The Passover Plot* (London: Hutchinson & Co., 1965), 132. Schonfield replicated the arguments and evidence of Heinrich E. G. Paulus, *Das Leben Jesu* (Heidelberg: D. F. Winter, 1828), Vol. II, Part I, 3 ff.

14. See, for example, Rudolf Bultmann, *Theology of the New Testament*, trans. Kendrick Grobel (New York: Charles Scribner's Sons, 1951), 1: 292–306; Günther Bornkamm, *Jesus of Nazareth*, trans. Irene and Fraser McLuskey (New York: Harper & Brothers, 1960), 179–91; John Knox, *Jesus Lord and Christ* (New York: Harper & Brothers, 1958), 117–39 and 264–76, or Hugh Anderson, *Jesus and Christian Origins* (New York: Oxford University Press, 1964), 185–240.

15. For the history of the rationalistic approach to the resurrection and the miracles see Dawe, *No Orthodoxy but the Truth*, 106–35. Martin Dibelius and others in the Bultmann tradition have analyzed again the use of comparative mythology as a means of explaining miracle stories in the Gospels. However, the idea is one that has been a favorite of modern theology since the time of Hegel.

16. Even in the mediating Christology of Donald Baillie there is a basic commitment to dealing with the humanity of Jesus in ways commensu-

rate with contemporary understanding of what it means to be human. See "The End of Docetism" in his *God Was in Christ*, 11–20.

17. Wolfhart Pannenberg, *Jesus—God and Man*, 2d ed., trans. Lewis L. Wilkins and Duane A. Priebe (Philadelphia: Westminster Press, 1968), 88–106.

18. Bloch, *Das Prinzip Hoffnung*, 1412 (author's trans.). This is an idea that has influenced Moltmann and Pannenberg. The humanistic Marxist analysis that informs Bloch's assertion is to be differentiated from the traditionally negative Marxist position on religious visions of the future. Humanistic Marxism, while recognizing the projective character of religion, explicates a positive function for religious visions of the human future. Religion points to the future potential of humankind. Nowhere is this clearer, he argues, than in messianic religions. The phrase Bloch uses to describe this is *"Wachsender Menscheinsatz ins religiöse Geheimnis."*

19. Jürgen Moltmann, *The Theology of Hope*, trans. James W. Leitch (New York: Harper & Row, 1967), 17.

20. Forsyth, *The Person and Place of Jesus Christ*, 323–57.

21. Georg Wilhelm Friedrich Hegel, *Werke, Vorlesungen über die Philosophie der Religion, II*, ed. Eva Moldenhaurer and Karl Markus Michel (Frankfurt am Main: Suhrkamp Verlag, 1967), 17: 297ff.

22. Pannenberg, *Jesus—God and Man*, 106–14, et al.

23. James A. Cone, *A Black Theology of Liberation*, 218.

24. Ibid. 210.

25. The literature on this question is already large and complex. Critical and prophetic literature identifying and protesting patriarchy in church and theology is now being followed by a literature of constructive theology. The move toward Christological reconstruction may be seen in Rosemary Radford Ruether, *Sexism and God-Talk* (Boston: Beacon Press, 1983), 116–38.

26. Krister Stendahl, *The Bible and the Role of Women* (Philadelphia: Fortress Press, 1966).

27. Elisabeth Schüssler Fiorenza, *In Memory of Her* (New York: Crossroad, 1983), 41–64.

28. Mary Carroll Smith raises questions about the possibility of using the concept "kingdom" in a nonsexist reconstruction of theology because it implies the notion of domination. See her "Response," *Christ's Lordship and Religious Pluralism*, ed. Gerald H. Anderson and Thomas F. Stransky (Maryknoll: Orbis Books, 1981), 156–58. For an answer to this see Fiorenza, 110–30.

CHAPTER 3: JESUS AND THE KINGDOM OF GOD

1. Gerhard Ebeling, *Word and Faith*, trans. James W. Leitch (Philadelphia: Fortress Press, 1963), 288.

2. Schleiermacher seeks to guard against a Christology that pictures Jesus purely in the form of a moral example by the distinction he draws between attributing to Jesus "an examplary *(vorbildliche)* dignity" and what he terms "ideality" *(Urbildlichkeit)*. Jesus is the Redeemer not because of his power to hold before humankind a picture *(Vorbild)* of what humans may become but by his being the creative archetype *(Urbild)* who is able to empower this new being in those who have faith in him. See *The Christian Faith*, 93.2: 377–80. By contrast, neo-orthodox Christologies, such as that of Brunner, merge revelation and redemption into one event. See Emil Brunner, *Revelation and Reason*, trans. Olive Wyon (Philadelphia: Westminster Press, 1946), 20–42. This obscures a fundamental psychological problem. As human beings we are able to envisage possibilities that we do not have the power to fulfill. In all talk about Jesus as the disclosure of the human future, it is necessary to describe him as both the disclosure of that future and as the one who empowers participation in it.

3. Joël de Rosnay, "Evolution and Time," *Teilhard Review*, 5 (1970/1971): 4–21.

4. Søren Kierkegaard, *Training in Christianity*, trans. Walter Lowrie (Princeton: Princeton University Press, 1944), 131.

5. Karl Barth, *Church Dogmatics, II/2,* trans. G. W. Bromiley et al. (Edinburgh: T. & T. Clark, 1957), 177.

6. Jesus cannot be comprehended by the model of the avatar as found in Hindu tradition. The avatar is a being who descends to earth to bring the message of salvation needed in a particular age. Such an idea is inevitably attractive to those who are in dialogue with modern Hinduism. See, for example, Sri Aurobindo [Ghose] *Essays on the Gita* (Pondicherry: Sri Aurobindo Ashram, 1966), 131–69. A similar argument is advanced by some in dialogue with the Buddhist tradition who seek to interpret Jesus in terms of the notion of the bodhisattva. There is a fundamental difficulty in all such attempts, as Eliade has made clear in *Cosmos and History*, 51–137. Hindu and Buddhist conception are related to the notion of the world and human history as samsara, the never-ending cycle of birth-suffering-death. Christian faith is formulated in relationship to the conception of the world and human history as existing within a time frame characterized by a beginning and an end. The life, death, and resurrection of Jesus are epochal events of salvation, not only as the source of the new vision of human redemption but as the source of the new being actualized in redemption.

7. Pannenberg, *Jesus—God and Man*, 365–78.

8. Pierre Teilhard de Chardin, *The Phenomenon of Man*, trans. Bernard Wall (New York: Harper Torchbooks, 1959), 254–72.

9. Pierre Teilhard de Chardin, *The Future of Man*, trans. Norman Denny (New York: Harper Torchbooks, 1964), 272–323.
10. Teilhard, *The Phenomenon of Man*, 271.
11. Pannenberg, *Basic Questions in Theology*, 2:239.
12. Because the chapter divisions and content of the Westminster Confession have been changed in different ways by the churches that use it as a confessional document, it seemed best to cite it with the text and chapter divisions from the text of 1646, as found in Leith, *Creeds of the Churches*, 193–230.
13. Quoted from the translation found in Nadejda Gorodetzky, *The Humiliated Christ in Modern Russian Thought* (London: S.P.C.K., 1938), 164.
14. Pierre Teilhard de Chardin, *The Divine Milieu*, trans. Bernard Wall (New York: Harper & Brothers, Publishers, 1960), 89, 104.

CHAPTER 4: THE DEATH OF JESUS
AS THE DISCLOSURE OF GOD

1. The *Confession of 1967* is unique in making central to its view of the work of Christ this multiplicity of images and metaphors rather than in selecting one of them to be given centrality, as did earlier Reformed confessions. Compare the *Confession of 1967*, 1.A.1 to Westminster Confession, 11.1–3.
2. A good example of these attempts to argue in a partly historical and partly systematic fashion for the priority of one particular type of atonement doctrine is that of Gustaf Aulén, *Christus Victor*, trans. A. G. Hebert (London: S.P.C.K., 1931). Yet Aulén was such a careful historian that he sensed the ambiguity of all such arguments. See 175–76.
3. No one has doubted the reality of Jesus' existence as a real flesh and blood human being since the defeat of docetism by the early church. Yet in 1948, Donald Baillie could still speak of the importance of the struggle against docetism. This was no longer the crass docetism of the ancient Gnostic teachers but the more subtle psychological docetism that subsumes Jesus' intellectual and spiritual life under the omniscience of the divine nature. Baillie argues for *"the human character of our Lord's moral and religious life"* (italics his), in *God Was in Christ*, 14. Many mediating theologians have looked to some doctrine of the divine self-limitation as a way of dealing with this problem. See Dawe, *The Form of a Servant*, 178–79.
4. Martin Rist, "Apocalypticism," *Interpreter's Dictionary of the Bible*, 1: 157–61. H. Ringgren, et al., "Apokalyptik," *Die Religion in Geschichte und Gegenwart* (Tübingen: J.C.B. Mohr, 1958), 1:463–72. R. H. Charles, *Eschatology* (New York: Schocken Books, 1963).
5. For an analysis of the reinterpretation of the apocalyptic in contemporary theologies of the future see Dawe, "Christology in Contemporary Systematic Theology," *Interpretation* 26, 266–69.

6. Joseph Campbell, *The Hero with a Thousand Faces* (Princeton: Princeton University Press, 1968), 3–48. Eliade, *Cosmos and History*, 27–48, 102–47. Ernest Becker, *The Denial of Death* (New York: The Free Press, 1973), 255–85.
7. Gerhard van der Leeuw, *Religion in Essence & Manifestation*, trans. J.E. Turner (London: George Allen & Unwin, Ltd., 1938), 664.
8. Eliade, *Cosmos and History*, 141–47.
9. Jürgen Moltmann, *The Crucified God*, trans. R. A. Wilson and John Bowden (New York: Harper & Row, 1974), 119. See also Rudolf Weth, "Heil im gekreuzigten Gott," *Evangelische Theologie*, 31 (1971): 227–44.
10. Augustine *City of God* 13. 3; *Contra Julian* 3. 24; et al.
11. Schwarz-Bart has given the legend of the *lamedvovniks*, the hidden saints who were responsible for the fate of the world, fresh currency as an interpretation of the Holocaust in his novel *The Last of the Just* (New York: Atheneum Publishers, 1960). The tradition of the thirty-six righteous men who will see the divine presence is found in the Babylonian Talmud, Sanh. 97b and Suk. 45b. In the Hasidic legends of the *lamedvovniks*, one of these figures appears at the moment of extremity to defeat the enemies of Israel. In light of the Holocaust, Schwarz-Bart reinterprets the legend into the account of a succession of martyrs.
12. Moltmann, *The Crucified God*, 128–45.
13. Paul Lehmann, *The Transfiguration of Politics* (New York: Harper & Row, 1975), 23–70.
14. Paul Tillich, *Systematic Theology*, 3 vols. (Chicago: University of Chicago Press, 1951, 1957, 1963), 1:140; 2:153.

CHAPTER 5: JESUS AND THE HISTORY OF GOD

1. Thomas Aquinas, *Summa Theologica*, Q. 10, Art. 2. The translation is from Anton C. Pegis, ed., *Basic Writings of Saint Thomas Aquinas* (New York: Random House, 1945), 1: 76.
2. Henry F. Lyte, "Abide With Me." *The Hymnbook* (Richmond: Presbyterian Church, U.S., et al., 1955), 54.
3. This line of thought comes into modern theology through Schleiermacher. See 50: 194 of *The Christian Faith:* "All attributes which we ascribe to God are to be taken as denoting not something special in God, but only something special in the manner in which the feeling of absolute dependence is to be related to him."
4. For an explication of this difficulty see Pannenberg, *Basic Questions in Theology*, 1: 15–80.
5. The theological implications of this historical development are derived by Patrick D. Miller, Jr., "God and the Gods," *Affirmation*, 1. 5 (1973): 37–62, and his *The Divine Warrior in Early Israel* (Cambridge, Mass.: Harvard University Press, 1973), 170 ff. Further work detailing the emergence of biblical monotheism is found in Hans-Peter Müller, "Gott

und die Götter in den Anfänger der biblischen Religion," *Monotheismus im Alten Israel und seiner Umwelt*, ed. Othmar Keel (Fribourg: Verlag Schweizerisches Katholisches Bibelwerk, 1980), 99–142.

6. Pannenberg grasps this idea clearly when he says that God is present "not only as the author of historical change . . . but also as the power for altering his own previous manifestations." *Basic Questions in Theology*, 2:114.

7. For guidance on this question in this complex literature see Sarvepalli Radhakrishnan, *The Principal Upanisads* (George Allen & Unwin, Ltd., 1968), 52–72 and Arthur B. Keith, *The Religion and Philosophy of the Veda and Upanishads* (Cambridge, Mass.: Harvard University Press, 1925), 516–29.

8. Donald G. Dawe, "Christian Faith in a Religiously Plural World," *Christian Faith in a Religiously Plural World*, ed. Donald G. Dawe and John B. Carman (Maryknoll: Orbis Books, 1978), 13–33.

9. Cyril of Alexandria, "The Epistle of Cyril to Nestorius With the XII Anathemas," *Migne Patrilogiae Graeque*, 77. 113 (author's trans.). For a recent translation, see Lionel Wickeham, *Cyril of Alexandria—Selected Letters* (Oxford: Clarendon Press, 1983), 12 ff.

10. Charles Hartshorne, *Man's Vision of God* (Chicago: Willett, Clark & Co., 1941), 1–56, and *Reality As Social Process* (Glencoe, Ill.: The Free Press, 1953), 155–62.

11. Barth, *Church Dogmatics*, II/1:496.

12. The use of "love" and "freedom" as basic definitions of the divine perfections is dependent on Barth, *Church Dogmatics* II/1, section 28. Unless these terms are defined in relationship to one another they lapse into a misleading natural theology of God as arbitrary power or of impotent longing.

13. Anselm, "Proslogium," chap. 7, *Basic Writings*, trans. Sidney Norton Deane (La Salle, Ill.: The Open Court Publishing Co., 1944), 12–13.

14. Goldenberg, *Changing of the Gods*, 28 ff.

CHAPTER 6: THE RESURRECTION OF
JESUS AS THE DISCLOSURE OF THE HUMAN

1. The notion of an exaltation of Jesus to a new and higher status by his resurrection is one with which theologians have had the greatest difficulty. The tendency since the time of the anti-Arian controversies is to follow the lead of such exegetes as Victorinus Afer and Athanasius (c. 296–373). They conceive of the resurrection-exaltation of Jesus as the disclosure of an abiding status he had that had been obscured during his time of exinanition. While their line of argumentation was cogent in the struggle against the Arians, it overlooked a good deal of New Testament evidence to the contrary. See Dawe, *The Form of a Servant*, 29–46.

2. Søren Kierkegaard, *Philosophical Fragments*, 74–93.

3. The reintroduction of serious consideration of the theological meaning of the empty tomb and the appearances is grounded in the work of Wolfhart Pannenberg, *Jesus—God and Man*, 88–106.

4. Van der Leeuw, *Religion in Essence & Manifestation*, 681.

5. Hans von Campenhausen, *Der Ablauf der Osterereignisse und das leere Grab* (Heidelberg: C. Winter, 1958), 31 ff.

6. T. F. Torrance (b. 1913) has done basic work in the reorientation of theology in relation to modern physics. He gives a methodological summary of his position in *Reality and Evangelical Theology* (Philadelphia: Westminster Press, 1982), 9–83. His more detailed work on this is found in his *Space, Time and Incarnation* (New York: Oxford University Press, 1969) and *Space, Time and Resurrection* (Grand Rapids, Mich.: Wm. B. Eerdmans Publishing Co., 1976).

7. The difficulty of modern exegesis in seeing the appearances as revelation of the new possibilities for human existence is seen in Raymond E. Brown, *The Gospel According to John, (XIII–XXI)*, Anchor Bible (Garden City: Doubleday & Co., 1970), 1033–36. Brown concludes that the story of Thomas and his insistence on touching the body of Jesus is to be explained as a "secondary elaboration" of the basic appearance narrative.

8. This analysis of the term "body" was introduced into modern theological discourse through the Old Testament studies of Johannes Pedersen, *Israel*, trans. Aslaug Møller (London: Oxford University Press, 1926), 1–2:99 ff. The development of this understanding of "body" in Paul is in John A. T. Robinson, *The Body* (Chicago: Henry Regnery Co., 1952).

9. The fulfillment of matter through its sanctification comes to expression in modern Western theology through Pierre Teilhard de Chardin. See for example, *Hymn of the Universe*, trans. Simon Bartholomew (New York: Harper & Row, 1965), 13–71. However, the divinization or sanctification of matter has been a major theme in the theologies of the Eastern churches. Vladimir Lossky, *The Mystical Theology of the Eastern Church* (Crestwood, N.Y.: St. Vladimir's Seminary Press, 1976), 196–216. John Meyendorff, *Byzantine Theology* (New York: Fordham University Press, 1974), 129–37.

10. John Hick takes a very different position in his analysis of the metaphors of salvation in these traditions. He argues that all symbols of ultimate salvation have a unified character. See his book *Death and Eternal Life* (New York: Harper & Row, 1976), 399–466. Despite his evident good will, he distorts these traditions in the interest of supporting his unitary theology of religion. See my article "Salvation," *Abingdon Dictionary of Living Religions*, 643–46.

11. Reinhold Niebuhr (1892–1971) gives careful analysis of the paradox of continuity and discontinuity in the New Testament teachings on resurrection. He says of 2 Cor. 5:4, KJV, "not ... unclothed, but clothed

upon": "In that succinct phrase the Biblical hope of a consummation which will sublimate rather than annul the whole historical process is perfectly expressed." See *Nature and Destiny of Man*, 2 vols. (New York: Charles Scribner's Sons, 1941–43), 2:298.

PART II: A TRANSITION POINT

1. The papers presented at this seminar were subsequently published in Harbans Singh, ed., *Perspectives on Guru Nanak* (Patiala: Guru Gobind Singh Department of Religious Studies, Punjabi University, 1975).
2. Karl Barth, *Church Dogmatics, I/2*, 280.
3. H. Richard Niebuhr, *The Meaning of Revelation* (New York: The Macmillan Co., 1941), 93.

CHAPTER 7: FAITH IN JESUS CHRIST

1. This terminology is from the phenomenological analysis of revelation in Paul Tillich, *Systematic Theology*, 1: 115–8. However, my use of these terms is not strictly Tillichian but reflects the phenomenology of religion in Gerhard van der Leeuw, 23–26, 679–89.
2. David Tracy, *Blessed Rage for Order*, 91–118.
3. David Hume, *Enquiries Concerning the Human Understanding*, ed. L. A. Selby-Bigge, 2d ed. (Oxford: Clarendon Press, 1902), Section X, 109–31. Flew shows this line of argumentation in Tillotson. See Anthony Flew, *Hume's Philosophy of Belief* (London: Routledge & Kegan Paul, 1961), 171–79.
4. Schleiermacher, *The Christian Faith*, 14:68.
5. Rudolf Bultmann, "New Testament and Mythology," in *Kerygma and Myth*, 28.
6. The literature on the relationship of Christianity to Buddhism is already very large. It ranges all the way from the speculative, pseudohistory of Arthur Lillie's *The Influence of Buddhism on Primitive Christianity* (New York: Charles Scribner's Sons, 1893) or Swami Satyananda, *The Origin of Christianity* (Calcutta: L. Chakraberty, 1923) that see Christianity as the reappearance of a form of Buddhism, to the more chastened and historical works such as those of Winston Lee King, *Buddhism and Christianity: Some Bridges of Understanding* (Philadelphia: Westminster Press, 1962), or D. T. Niles' sensitive rethinking of the Christian mission to Buddhists in *Buddhism and the Claims of Christ* (Richmond: John Knox Press, 1967). The characteristic note struck in the contemporary literature on the so-called "Eastern religions" is that of D. T. Suzuki, *Mysticism: Buddhist and Christian* (New York: Harper and Row, 1957), who argues that when stripped of institutional and doctrinal accretions, the mystical tradition in Christianity and Buddhism is identical. A far more perceptive vision of this question is found in Mahinda Palihawadana, "A Buddhist Response: Religion Beyond Ideology and

Power," *Christian Faith in a Religiously Plural World*, 34–45. As travel to the East has become easier, there have been a number of traveling theologians, from Canon A. N. Streeter to Paul Tillich and Dom Aelrad Graham, who have reflected on personal encounters with Buddhism. While motivated by evident good will, they have not illuminated the difficult issues of the relationship of Christianity and Buddhism.

7. Ernst Troeltsch, *The Absoluteness of Christianity and the History of Religions*, trans. David Reid (Richmond: John Knox Press, 1971), 131 ff. Near the end of his life, Troeltsch became convinced that his position was no longer tenable and retreated from this line of apologetic argument. See his "Christianity Among World Religions," *Christian Thought: Its History and Applications*, ed. Baron F. von Huegel (New York: Meridian Books, 1957), 35–63.

8. Morton Smith, *The Secret Gospel* (New York: Harper & Row, 1973), 104–8, *Clement of Alexandria and a Secret Gospel of Mark* (Cambridge, Mass.: Harvard University Press, 1973), 220–37. Early Christian apologetics dealt with Jewish and pagan claims that Jesus was a magician. See Justin, *First Apology* 30; *Dialogue* 69.7; Origen *Contra Celsum* 1.6; Tertullian *Apology* 21.17; Arnobius *Adversus Nationes* 1.43. The Babylonian Talmud reports on Jesus as a magician. See *B. Sanhedrin* 43a; and in *B. Sanhedrin* 107b and *B. Sotah* 47a. Jesus is pictured as a pupil of Rabbi Joshua ben Perahyah, who was known for his work as a magician.

9. Van der Leeuw, *Religion in Essence & Manifestation*, 681–82.

10. Ibid., 23, 28. Michael Gilsenan, *Recognizing Islam* (New York: Pantheon Books, 1982), 75–87.

11. Dawe, "Christology in Contemporary Theology," *Interpretation* 26, 271–72.

12. Arthur Koestler coined this phrase in his popular treatment of this idea, *The Ghost in the Machine* (New York: Macmillan, 1967).

13. Baruch Spinoza saw the fallacy of finding God in the gaps in the structure of understanding in *Tractatus Theologico-politicus: A Theological and Political Treatise*, 2d ed. (London: N. Trubner & Co., 1868). The perception of the world as characterized by both order and contingency and the theological importance of that perception is given with great learning by Stanley Jaki, *The Road of Science and the Ways to God* (Chicago: University of Chicago Press, 1978), 246–96.

14. Paul Tillich, *Systematic Theology*, 3: 152–55.

15. Near the end of his life, Barth indicated his interest in eventually turning to the study of other religious traditions. He was never able to intimate even the lines this might follow, except for the brief account in *Church Dogmatics*, I/2: 340–44.

16. Hans Kung, "The World Religions in God's Plan of Salvation," *Christian Revelation and World Religions*, ed. Joseph Neuner (London: Burns & Oates, 1967), 51–3.

CHAPTER 8: JESUS AND THE WHOLE WORLD

1. Nikolaus von Kues, "De Pace Fedei," *Werke*, ed. Paul Wilpert (Berlin: Walter de Gruyter & Co., 1967), 1:338–66.
2. The question of how the Reformers related to the missionary movement is a complex one. Lutheran, Reformed, and Anglican teachers of the sixteenth century were centered on the problems of European Christendom with few exceptions. Only among the radical Reformers and the Anabaptists did the vision of a mission to the rest of the world start to take shape. See Hans Kasdorf, "The Reformation and Mission: A Bibliographical Survey of Secondary Literature," *Occasional Bulletin of Missionary Research* 4 (October, 1980): 169–75.
3. The importance of names in Hebrew thought has been shown by Pedersen, *Israel*, 1–2: 245–59. See also Raymond Abba, "Name," *The Interpreter's Dictionary of the Bible*, 3: 500–508.
4. Wilfred Cantwell Smith, "Is the Qur'an the Word of God?" *Questions of Religious Truth* (New York: Charles Scribner's Sons, 1967), 39–62.
5. Raimundo Panikkar, *The Unknown Christ of Hinduism*, new edition (London: Darton, Longman & Todd, 1981), 97–162.
6. The notion of revelation in Christ as the light to illumine the ambiguities of human religious life was suggested early in this century by John Nicol Farquhar in *The Crown of Hinduism* (New York: Oxford University Press, 1913). The illuminating power of revelation is at the heart of the doctrine of revelation as developed by H. Richard Niebuhr, *The Meaning of Revelation,* 93. Emil Brunner relates revelation in Christ to other religions in a very guarded fashion in his *Revelation and Reason*, 218–36.
7. Bede Griffiths, *Christ in India* (New York: Charles Scribner's Sons, 1966), 163–223, and Panikkar in *The Unknown Christ of Hinduism* have sought to clarify what it means to believe that Christ is already in all of the world. Cf., Heinrich Meyer, "Meeting Men of Other Faiths," *Witness in Six Continents*, ed. Ronald K. Orchard (Edinburgh: Edinburgh House Press, 1964), 104–5, and Carl E. Braaten, "The Christian Mission and American Imperialism," *Dialog* 15 (1976): 70–8. Not only have individual theologians affirmed the universal presence of Christ but so has the "Statement of the Theological Consultation on Dialogue in Community, Chiang Mai, Thailand," April 18–27, 1977, which was authorized by the Central Committee of the World Council of Churches. See *Occasional Bulletin of Missionary Research* 1:2 (April 1977): 27.
8. The foundational work for this functional approach to the question of orthodoxy and heresy was set forth in Schleiermacher, *The Christian Faith*, 20–31: 94–128.
9. Augustine *City of God* 5. 12 ff; 19. 25.

10. Wilfred Cantwell Smith, *Towards a World Theology* (Philadelphia: Westminster Press, 1981), 168.
11. Ibid., 172.
12. One of the most interesting examples of this is seen in the outcomes of the extensive Christian mission work in India. Not only Christian interpreters such as J. N. Farquhar but also Hindu scholars such as D. S. Sarma have pointed out how mission preaching called forth the response of renewal and humanization in Hindu life. See S. M. Pathak, *American Missionaries and Hinduism* (Delhi: Munshiram Manoharlal, 1967), 237–48, or K. L. Seshagiri Rao, *Mahatma Gandhi and C. F. Andrews* (Patiala: Punjabi University Press, 1969), 69–75.

Bibliography

Adam, Karl. *The Christ of Faith.* Translated by Joyce Crick. New York: New American Library, Mentor Omega Books, 1962.

Alves, Rubem A. *A Theology of Human Hope.* Washington: Corpus Books, 1969.

Anderson, Hugh. *Jesus and Christian Origins.* New York: Oxford University Press, 1964.

Anselm. *Basic Writings.* Translated by Sidney Norton Deane. La Salle, Ill.: The Open Court Publishing Co., 1944.

Aquinas, Thomas. *Basic Writings of Saint Thomas Aquinas.* Edited by Anton C. Pegis. New York: Random House, 1945.

Augustine. *The City of God.* Translated by Marcus Dods. 2 vols. New York: Hafner Publishing Company, 1948.

Aulén, Gustaf. *Christus Victor.* Translated by A. G. Hebert. London: S.P.C.K., 1931.

Aurobindo [Ghose] Sri. *Essays on the Gita.* Pondicherry: Sri Aurobindo Ashram, 1966.

Baillie, Donald. *God Was in Christ.* New York: Charles Scribner's Sons, 1948.

Bartsch, Hans, ed. *Kerygma and Myth.* Translated by Reginald Fuller. London: S.P.C.K., 1956.

Barth, Karl. *Church Dogmatics, II/2.* Translated by G. W. Bromiley. Edinburgh: T. & T. Clark, 1957.

Becker, Ernest. *The Denial of Death.* New York: The Free Press, 1973.

Bethune-Baker, J. F. *An Introduction to the Early History of Christian Doctrine.* London: Methun & Co., Ltd., 1903.

Bloch, Ernst. *Das Prinzip Hoffnung.* 2 vols. Frankfurt: Suhrkamp Verlag, 1959.

Bornkamm, Günther. *Jesus of Nazareth.* Translated by Irene and Fraser McLuskey. New York: Harper & Brothers, 1960.

Brown, Raymond E. *The Gospel According to John (XIII–XXI).* Anchor Bible. Garden City: Doubleday & Co., 1970.

Brunner, Emil. *Revelation and Reason.* Translated by Olive Wyon. Philadelphia: Westminster Press, 1946.

Bultmann, Rudolf. *Theology of the New Testament.* Translated by Kendrick Grobel. New York: Charles Scribner's Sons, 1951.

Buttrick, George A., ed. *The Interpreter's Dictionary of the Bible.* New York: Abingdon Press, 1962.

Calvin, John. *Institutes of the Christian Religion.* Translated by Ford Lewis Battles. Philadelphia: Westminster Press, 1960.

Campbell, Joseph. *The Hero with a Thousand Faces.* Princeton: Princeton University Press, 1968.

Childs, Brevard S. *Biblical Theology in Crisis.* Philadelphia: Westminster Press, 1970.

———. *Introduction to the Old Testament as Scripture.* Philadelphia: Fortress Press, 1979.

Cleage, Albert B., Jr. *The Black Messiah.* New York: Sheed and Ward, 1968.

Collingwood, R. G. *The Idea of History.* New York: Oxford University Press, 1946.

Cone, James H. *A Black Theology of Liberation.* Philadelphia: J. B. Lippincott Company, 1970.

Crim, Keith, ed. *Abingdon Dictionary of the Bible.* Nashville: Abingdon Press, 1981.

Cross, F. L. and Livingston, E. A. *The Oxford Dictionary of the Christian Church.* 2d ed. Oxford: Oxford University Press, 1974.

Daly, Mary. *Beyond God the Father.* Boston: Beacon Press, 1973.

Dawe, Donald G. *The Form of a Servant.* Philadelphia: Westminster Press, 1963.

———. *No Orthodoxy but the Truth.* Philadelphia: Westminster Press, 1969.

Dawe, Donald G., and Carman, John B., eds. *Christian Faith in a Religiously Plural World.* Maryknoll: Orbis Books, 1978.

Dorner, Isaak. *Entwicklungsgeschichte der Lehre von der Person Christi.* Stuttgart: 1839, 2d ed., 4 vols. 1846–56.

Ebeling, Gerhard. *Word and Faith.* Translated by James W. Leitch. Philadelphia: Fortress Press, 1963.

Edinger, Edward F. *Ego and Archetype.* New York: G. P. Putnam's Sons, 1972.

Eliade, Mircea. *Cosmos and History.* Translated by Willard R. Trask. New York: Harper Torchbooks, 1959.

Farquhar, John Nicol. *The Crown of Hinduism.* London: Oxford University Press, 1913.

Fiorenza, Elisabeth Schüssler. *In Memory of Her.* New York: Crossroad, 1983.

Flew, Anthony. *Hume's Philosophy of Belief.* London: Routledge & Kegan Paul, 1961.

Ford, Lewis S. *The Lure of God: A Biblical Background to Process Theism.* Philadelphia: Fortress Press, 1978.

Forsyth, P. T. *The Person and Place of Jesus Christ.* London: Congregational Union of England and Wales, 1909; reprint ed., Independent Press, 1955.

Foucault, Michel. *The Birth of the Clinic.* Translated by A. M. Sheridan Smith. New York: Vintage Books, 1973.

Gilsenan, Michael. *Recognizing Islam.* New York: Pantheon Books, 1982.

Goldenberg, Naomi R. *Changing of the Gods.* Boston: Beacon Press, 1979.

Gorodetzky, Nadejda. *The Humiliated Christ in Modern Russian Thought.* London: S.P.C.K., 1938.

Grabner-Haider, Anton, ed. *Die Bibel und unsere Sprache: Konkrete Hermeneutik.* Wien: Herder, 1970.

Griffin, David Ray. *A Process Christology.* Philadelphia: Westminster Press, 1973.

Griffiths, Bede. *Christ in India.* New York: Charles Scribner's Sons, 1966.

Hall, Stanley. *Jesus, the Christ, in the Light of Psychology.* New York: Doubleday, Page, & Company, 1917.

Hamilton, Neill. *Jesus for a No-God World.* Philadelphia: Westminster Press, 1969.

Hamilton, William, and Altizer, Thomas J. J. *Radical Theology and the Death of God.* Indianapolis: Bobbs-Merrill Co., 1966.

Hartshorne, Charles. *Man's Vision of God.* Chicago: Willett, Clark & Company, 1941.

――――. *Reality as Social Process.* Glencoe, Ill.: The Free Press, 1953.

Hastings, James, ed. *Encyclopaedia of Religion and Ethics.* New York: Charles Scribner's Sons, 1914.

Hick, John. *Death and Eternal Life.* New York: Harper & Row, 1976.

Hocking, William E., chair, Laymen's Foreign Mission Inquiry. Commission of Appraisal. *Re-thinking Missions: A Laymen's Inquiry After 100 Years.* New York: Harper & Brothers, 1932.

Hume, David. *Enquiries Concerning the Human Understanding.* Edited by L. A. Selby-Bigge. Oxford: Clarendon Press, 1902.

Jaki, Stanley. *The Road of Science and the Ways to God.* Chicago: University of Chicago Press, 1978.

Kant, Immanuel. *Critique of Practical Reason.* Translated by T. K. Abbott. London: Longmans, Green and Co., 1948.

Keel, Othmar, ed. *Monotheismus im Alten Israel und seiner Umwelt.* Fribourg: Verlag Schweizerisches Katholisches Bibelwerk, 1980.

Keith, Arthur B. *The Religion and Philosophy of the Veda and Upanishads.* Cambridge, Mass.: Harvard University Press, 1925.

Kelly, J. N. D. *Early Christian Doctrines,* 2d ed. London: Adam & Charles Black, 1960.

Kierkegaard, Søren. *Philosophical Fragments.* Translated by David F. Swenson. Princeton: Princeton University Press, 1936.

――――. *Training in Christianity.* Translated by Walter Lowrie. Princeton: Princeton University Press, 1944.

King, Winston Lee. *Buddhism and Christianity: Some Bridges of Understanding.* Philadelphia: Westminster Press, 1962.

Knox, John. *Jesus Lord and Christ.* New York: Harper & Brothers, 1958.

Koestler, Arthur. *The Ghost in the Machine.* New York: Macmillan, 1967.

Küng, Hans. *On Being a Christian.* Translated by Edward Quinn. Garden City: Doubleday & Co., 1976.

Lehmann, Paul. *The Transfiguration of Politics*. New York: Harper & Row, 1975.

Leith, John H., ed. *Creeds of the Churches*. 3d ed. Atlanta: John Knox Press, 1982.

Lessing, Gotthold Ephraim. *Gesammelte Werke*. edited by Paul Rilla. Berlin: Aufbau Verlag, 1956.

Lillie, Arthur. *The Influence of Buddhism on Primitive Christianity*. New York: Charles Scribner's Sons, 1893.

Lorenz, Konrad. *On Aggression*. Translated by Marjorie K. Wilson. New York: Harcourt, Brace & World, 1966.

Lossky, Vladimir. *The Mystical Theology of the Eastern Church*. Crestwood, N.Y.: St. Vladimir's Seminary Press, 1976.

Martin, Malachi. *Jesus Now*. New York: E. P. Dutton & Co., Inc., 1973.

McGarry, Michael B., C.S.P. *Christology After Auschwitz*. New York: Paulist Press, 1977.

Meyendorff, John. *Byzantine Theology*. New York: Fordham University Press, 1974.

Miller, Patrick D., Jr. *The Divine Warrior in Early Israel*. Cambridge,Mass.: Harvard University Press, 1973.

Moltmann, Jürgen. *The Crucified God*. Translated by R. A. Wilson and John Bowden. New York: Harper & Row, Publishers, 1974.

––––––. *The Theology of Hope*. Translated by James W. Leitch. New York: Harper & Row, 1967.

Neuner, Joseph, ed. *Christian Revelation and World Religions*. London: Burns & Oates, 1967.

Niebuhr, H. Richard. *The Meaning of Revelation*. New York: The Macmillan Company, 1941.

Niebuhr, Reinhold. *The Nature and Destiny of Man*. 2 vols. New York: Charles Scribner's Sons, 1941–43.

Niles, D. T. *Buddhism and the Claims of Christ*. Richmond: John Knox Press, 1967.

Orchard, Ronald K. *Witness in Six Continents*. Edinburgh: House Press, 1954.

Panikkar, Raimundo. *The Unknown Christ of Hinduism*. Rev. ed. London: Darton, Longman & Todd, 1964.

Pannenberg, Wolfhart. *Basic Questions in Theology*. 2 vols. Translated by George H. Kehm. Philadelphia: Fortress Press, 1970–71.

––––––. *Jesus—God and Man*. 2d ed. Translated by Lewis L. Wilkins and Duane A. Priebe. Philadelphia: Westminster Press, 1968.

––––––. *What Is Man? Contemporary Anthropology in Theological Perspective*. Translated by Duane A. Priebe. Philadelphia: Fortress Press, 1970.

Pathak, S. M. *American Missionaries and Hinduism*. Delhi: Munshiram Manoharlal, 1967.

Paulus, E. G. *Das Leben Jesus*. Heidelberg: D. F. Winter, 1828.

Pedersen, Johannes. *Israel.* Translated by Aslaug Møller. London: Oxford University Press, 1926.

Perrin, Norman. *Rediscovering the Teachings of Jesus.* London: S.C.M. Press, 1957.

Prestige, Leonard. *God in Patristic Thought.* London: S.P.C.K., 1952.

Radhakrishnan, Sarvepalli. *The Principal Upanisads.* London: George Allen & Unwin, Ltd., 1968.

Rao, K. L. Seshagiri. *Mahatma Gandhi and C. F. Andrews.* Patiala: Punjabi University Press, 1969.

Robinson, John A. T. *The Body.* Chicago: Henry Regnery Co., 1952.

Rosenzweig, Franz. *Briefe und Tagebücher.* Edited by Edith Rosenzweig. Berlin: Shocken Verlag, 1935.

Ruether, Rosemary Radford. *Sexism and God-Talk.* Boston: Beacon Press, 1983.

Satyananda, Swami. *The Origin of Christianity.* Calcutta: L. Chakraberty, 1923.

Schleiermacher, Friedrich. *The Christian Faith.* Edited by H. R. Mackintosh and J. S. Stewart. Edinburgh: T. & T. Clark, 1928.

Schonfield, Hugh J. *The Passover Plot.* London: Hutchinson & Co., 1965.

Schwarz-Bart, Andre. *The Last of the Just.* New York: Atheneum Publishers, 1960.

Schweitzer, Albert. *The Quest of the Historical Jesus.* Translated by W. Montgomery. New York: The Macmillan Company, 1955.

Singh, Harbans, ed. *Perspectives on Guru Nanak.* Patiala: Guru Gobind Singh Department of Religious Studies, Punjabi University, 1975.

Smith, Morton. *Clement of Alexandria and a Secret Gospel of Mark.* Cambridge, Mass.: Harvard University Press, 1973.

————. *The Secret Gospel.* New York: Harper & Row, 1973.

Smith, Wilfred Cantwell. *Questions of Religious Truth.* New York: Charles Scribner's Sons, 1957.

————. *Towards a World Theology.* Philadelphia: Westminster Press, 1981.

Sobrino, Jon, S.J. *Christology at the Crossroads.* Translated by John Drury. Maryknoll: Orbis Books, 1978.

Sölle, Dorothee. *Christ the Representative.* Translated by David Lewis. Philadelphia: Fortress Press, 1967.

Spinoza, Baruch. *Tractatus Theologico-politicus: A Theological and Political Treatise,* ... 2d ed. London: N. Trubner & Co., 1868.

Steiner, George. *After Babel.* New York: Oxford University Press, 1975.

Suzuki, D. T. *Mysticism: Buddhist and Christian.* New York: Harper & Row, 1957.

Teilhard de Chardin, Pierre. *The Divine Milieu.* Translated by Bernard Wall. New York: Harper & Brothers, Publishers, 1960.

————. *The Future of Man.* Translated by Norman Denny. New York: Harper Torchbooks, 1964.

————. *The Phenomenon of Man.* Translated by Bernard Wall. New York: Harper Torchbooks, 1959.

Thunberg, Lars. *Microcosm and Mediator.* Lund: C. W. K. Gleerup, 1965.

Tillich, Paul. *Systematic Theology.* 3 vols. Chicago: University of Chicago Press, 1951, 1957, 1963.

Torrance, Thomas F. *Reality and Evangelical Theology.* Philadelphia: Westminster Press, 1982.

————. *Space, Time and Incarnation.* New York: Oxford University Press, 1969.

Tracy, David. *Blessed Rage for Order.* New York: Seabury Press, 1975.

Troeltsch, Ernst. *The Absoluteness of Christianity and the History of Religions.* Translated by David Reid. Richmond: John Knox Press, 1971.

————. *Christian Thought: Its History and Applications.* Edited by Baron F. von Huegel. New York: Meridian Books, 1957.

————. *Der Historismus und seine Probleme,* in *Gesammelte Schriften.* 3 vols. Tübingen: Verlag von J. C. B. Mohr, 1922.

Tucker, Robert. *Philosophy and Myth in Karl Marx.* Cambridge: Cambridge University Press, 1965.

Van Buren, Paul M. *The Secular Meaning of the Gospel.* New York: Macmillan, 1963.

Van der Leeuw, Gerhard. *Religion in Essence & Manifestation.* 2 vols. Translated by J. E. Turner. London: George Allen & Unwin, Ltd., 1938.

Von Campenhausen, Hans. *Der Ablauf der Osterereignisse und das leere Grab.* Heidelberg: C. Winter, 1958.

————. *Die Religion in Geschichte und Gegenwart.* 3 vols. Tübingen: Verlag von J. C. B. Mohr & Co., 1957–62.

Von Kues, Nikolaus. *Werke.* Edited by Paul Wilpert. Berlin: Walter de Gruyter & Co., 1957.

Welch, Claude, ed. *God and Incarnation in Mid-nineteenth Century German Theology.* New York: Oxford University Press, 1965.

Werner, Martin. *The Formation of Christian Dogma.* Translated by S. G. F. Brandon. New York: Harper & Brothers, 1957.

Wetter, Gustav A. *Dialectical Materialism.* Translated by Peter Heath. New York: Frederick A. Praeger, 1959.

Wickeham, Lionel, ed. and trans. *Cyril of Alexandria—Selected Letters.* Oxford: Clarendon Press, 1983.

Wickler, Wolfgang. *The Biology of the Ten Commandments.* Translated by David Smith. New York: McGraw-Hill Book Co., 1972.

Wolfson, Harry Austryn. *The Philosophy of the Church Fathers.* 2d ed. Cambridge, Mass.: Harvard University Press, 1964.

Index of Names and Subjects

Index of Scripture References